The Poetry of Delmore Schwartz

The Poetry of Delmore Schwartz

by
Robert H. Deutsch

Edited by John N. Serio

The Wallace Stevens Society Press
Potsdam, N.Y.

Published by
The Wallace Stevens Society Press
Clarkson University P.O. Box 5750
Potsdam, NY 13699
www.wallacestevens.com

In collaboration with
Waxwing Editions
171 Pier Avenue, #339
Santa Monica, CA 90405
www.waxwingeditions.com

Series editor John N. Serio
Cover by Kathryn Jacobi

Library of Congress Control Number: 2003100863

ISBN 0-9648056-3-4 (pbk.)

Printed on recycled paper.

CONTENTS

INTRODUCTION

It is not easy to appraise a contemporary writer of stature. There are real grounds for the fact that full-scale appraisals increase in number after a writer's death. If the critic respects his contemporary who, as in this case, may have been a good poet, he must assume that, in regard to the experience of his time and place, the poet was involved at least as deeply as the critic. Yet it is the critic's job to conquer the meaningfulness of the poet, covering, indeed, the very complex of experience that the poet could only fully express in the complete body of his poetry. To accomplish this for the discursive level, the critic must seek a point of transcendency, a conceptual vantage point, an intellectual angle, the excellence of which is directly proportionate to its comprehensiveness, everything else remaining equal. After the poet's death, when sufficient time has elapsed, such points of transcendence or inclusion present themselves. They are gifts of time, of the motion of the culture. It is often said that an author's death arrests the change that otherwise continues to occur in his earlier work through the production of later work, thus affording the critic a picture that remains comparatively static.

Just as the critic tries to achieve a point of transcendency, so the poet reaches for as wide a level of inclusion as possible. There is a creative crest of the wave for any particular period or time, one that a writer must reach and from which he must write if he is to make a bid for major stature. To reach this point, he must include the experience of his age, and from this point almost anything he writes must be of significance. It is just one, merely a *single* stance, but from it come all the comments and corrections of a major writer. Many perfectly good, minor craftsmen write from other levels, but the major writer's work develops an ultimate comment for his time, but one that, nevertheless, is fundamental.

It is for this reason that T. S. Eliot evokes and sustains so much consideration. Delmore Schwartz, for his time, seemed to be such a one. So far as comparison is concerned, Eliot in many ways may be taken as Schwartz's polar opposite. Eliot believed in God; Schwartz, although he occasionally said he believed, did not give evidence of believing in even doubt. Eliot emphasized the impersonal and achieved the essence of the personal; Schwartz emphasized the personal and reached the ultimate loss of self. Eliot is the classicist; Schwartz the romantic. Eliot embraced faith and made of his belief a structure for poetry; Schwartz rejected faith and the rejection drowned his religious feeling in secularity. Eliot developed an ordered intellectual center (a different affair from belief) and produced a body of work celebrating order, while Schwartz, it seems, avoiding such commitment, depended on his sensibility and, in the end, produced work celebrating disorder.

Nevertheless, Schwartz was one of the half-dozen best poets of a generation that included Randall Jarrell, Robert Lowell, John Berryman, and Theodore Roethke. Although his first book gained considerable recognition, this was not the case with his subsequent work. Schwartz gave promise of depth and breadth of greatness. But something happened. The tight poetic line, the incisive and striking phrasing of his early poetry loosened as time passed and grew vague, repetitive, and amorphous. Yet Schwartz thought of himself as a great poet, and many agreed, at least on the fact that he had potential. Wallace Stevens, for instance, thought he was the most talented of the younger poets. And so the poetry of Delmore Schwartz stands as an anomaly, presenting several interesting problems that an analysis based on a consideration of his work in chronological order will help to solve.

The corpus of Schwartz's work makes only the slightest bow to tradition. It is as if competing clarities invite the reader's rejection on the ground that the whole carnival of attitudes roams his pages like a group of nomads—without the architecture of home. No order but the order of discovery seemed appropriate for handling a writer who, although refusing to fall easily into a tradition, was too sophisticated to be called primitive. The handling of such a problem appears to be a straightforward examination of his books of poetry in the order in which they were published.

It is foolish to deny that literary clues are not biographical clues; of course they are. But many critics have found it helpful to keep the one level separate from the other as much as possible. In the case of Delmore Schwartz, however, the poet's "position" is almost his only theme. The very first encounter with the first poem in his first book brought the author himself, poorly hidden behind layers of masks, violently into prominence. For this reason, theme was emphasized at the outset. Schwartz's first book, *In Dreams Begin Responsibilities*, begins with the poem "Coriolanus and His Mother: The Dream of One Performance." The order of discovery demanded an answer to the question: why Coriolanus? A single reading showed the strong identification of the author with Coriolanus. It only remained to trace down clue after clue and to use each one as a nail with which to pin the author to his true persona, Coriolanus. I say "true" because Schwartz uses a projection of himself as well in the poem. Therefore, each separate investigation, each clue, is important and the total has established, beyond doubt I think, an interesting picture of certain tendencies in Schwartz himself. What emerges is the portrait of a narcissist, a perfectionist, an image-maker, rigid, impenetrable, uncompromising. On the surface, Schwartz exhibited no such traits, particularly later on in life, but the young man possessed all of them and, of course, more. About his art, Schwartz was always serious, and a serious young poet must fight for purity in his work. "Coriolanus and His Mother," however, demonstrates almost an obsessive preoccupation with the theme. Schwartz, in fact, states it explicitly; there was little need to dig it out. The only digging that occurred was in the effort to show his identification with his main character and this was hardly difficult since he refers to Coriolanus as "my twin."

Although the consideration of theme is paramount in the more or less introductory study of "Coriolanus and His Mother," the structural device used in the poem—the same device exploited in his first short story, which is not analyzed here because of its genre—reveals, at this very beginning of his life as a poet, Schwartz's interest in defensive masking. He offers the poem as a dream of the author in which he sees himself attending a performance of a play resembling Shakespeare's *Coriolanus* and participating in it and commenting on it. Note the levels—Schwartz's dreaming of himself commenting on himself commenting. There are personae within personae, masks within masks.

This was the second time this defensive, self-conscious split was used in his first book. The device itself points up the author's supreme distrust, an alertness based on suspicion, and a suspicion that demanded defense. This is the more or less self-imposed isolation from which Schwartz issued all his poems, almost as if they were communiqués in the battle between his selves and the rest of humankind. Bit by bit, these revelations added up to the explanation that seemed, finally, to account for the direction taken in his later work.

The second section of *In Dreams Begin Responsibilities,* the eleven poems written, as Schwartz said, "In Imitation of the Fugue Form," reveals other aspects of the poet. The basic, fugal subject is on the level of the theme, and the theme is "no solace." Schwartz's frantic shuttling between the poles of the real and the ideal, good and evil, acceptance and rejection again demonstrates his powerful urge to settle into a unified whole that contained everything. He was not satisfied to submit the partial, which submission to a tradition seemed to mean to him. Other themes that concerned him are shown to be corollary; they are other windows in the same house (although the reader's light falls upon them from different angles at different times). This set of poems takes up, in turn, each aspect of life, which one way or another might be considered a solace, and shows how ineffective it is, specifically, and how illusory is the general notion of solace. The poet treated love, freedom of will, length of life, friendship, emotions, the joys of the body, the strengths of the ego, and companionship. None of these distract, says Schwartz, even from distraction.

In the part of the book devoted to separate lyrics, the same themes are repeated and others added. The lyrics are concerned with the power of the past, one's forebears. They present Schwartz's own powerful and complex self-consciousness, his need to set watchers watching the watchers, and, finally, his basic interest in rendering the moment-to-moment sense of being-in-the-world. All of this is the picture of an exacerbated sensibility momentarily saved by preoccupation with the writing of poetry. The refuge for Schwartz was in the aesthetic and not once is *this* "solace" mentioned in "The Repetitive Heart," which is eleven poems "In Imitation of the Fugue Form," in which he destroys each illusion through which men seek solace. Schwartz defensively separates himself from a complete account of his total situation here just as he does in all his work. He makes himself the viewer, and the viewer transcends. But the final problem of the viewer is never touched or treated and, in the end, both in his literary world and in the real world, he must lose for lack of succor. No more than he could submit to literary tradition could Schwartz accept a single, ordering belief. His discussion of this is presented in "Dr. Bergen's Belief," a closet drama that ends this first volume.

The remaining books bring into greater clarity two basic problems. How is it that Schwartz, one of whose basic aims was to offer a sense of being that is a matter of the greatest intimacy and recency, proffers work that somehow seems dated? And what brought about the loosening in his last work? The idea of "focus" helps explain the first matter. Study showed that there is a distance between Schwartz and his object at all times, and these poles were really much farther apart than is the custom today. The theory of focus entails a description of the shift in the sense of reality since Descartes. This is a coming together of the subjective and the objective.

Poets, today, write with shorter focus on the world and hence their subject matter than they did heretofore. The shorter the focus, the closer the subject matter until, finally, the emphasis is on the subject that, in a sense, becomes the object. Simply, Schwartz did not use commensurate means for rendering the sense of intimacy, means that are available to contemporary poets. He remained, stylistically, at a Cartesian distance—the elliptical, the irrational, the abridgement of syntactical convention, these means and more were never used by Schwartz, the rationalist.

The second problem that relates to the change in the quality of his poetry is more closely connected with his development of themes, and the analysis of these helps to resolve it. *Vaudeville for a Princess* finally reveals itself not so much as a bridge between the early and late work—although this is, to an extent, the case—but as a desperate attempt to shore up the author's last defenses: in it the use of strict form masks the tendency to overflow or fall apart. It proves to be a mask of calm and objectivity, and Schwartz even discusses this matter of donning or stripping off masks in one of his poems in this book. But these defenses could not contain the fullness of the poet.

In *Summer Knowledge* the dikes are down and the world floods Schwartz because the poet knew no limits and would accept neither the constraint of tradition nor of belief. As he covered a wider range of reality, it was natural that his rationalistic mode could express the inexpressible only by widening the poles of his paradoxes until the separation produced only the general, the vague, the amorphous. Schwartz thus moved steadily in the direction of exultant and mystical affirmation expressed in long, incantatory lines, the content of which is, nevertheless, banal. The poems in this last volume demonstrated not what they appear at first to say, namely that the author has finally dropped his hostility in favor of love, but only that he retains his mask until the end. But now the face of the mask has changed; it implies a giving-over, an acceptance that the poet knew was a possible salvation but which, in truth, he could not accept. This difference between pretense and reality is apparent in the continued cynicism and the gaseous effusions of the poetic line.

The fault, one finally sees, lies in one place and is there from the beginning. The child, as revealed in the autobiographical poem *Genesis,* suffered through his parents' unhappy marriage and grew to distrust everything. This accounts for the frantic need for awareness upon awareness and for the feeling of separateness that was a defense. It also accounts for Schwartz's reliance on rational systems at a time when poets were achieving the very intimacy he sought by a comparative abandonment of such dependence. Most significantly damaging, however, was Schwartz's mode of knowing—consumption, incorporation without direction or limitation, a natural outgrowth of distrust. He identified everything with himself, and he moved to immediate inclusion. This buttressed his ego even through all his poetic exorcisms to the contrary.

Delmore Schwartz ended having only affirmation to affirm. Although he ostensibly gave up his distrust, his poetic style belied this at the very same time that it revealed a deteriorating poetry.

First Poems 1939–1948

IN DREAMS BEGIN RESPONSIBILITIES

Separate Lyrics

Delmore Schwartz was graduated from high school in 1930—an exceptionally good year for poetry. Ezra Pound published *A Draft of 30 Cantos*; T. S. Eliot, *Poems 1909–1925*; Hart Crane, *The Bridge*; and Conrad Aiken, *John Deth*. Shortly afterward, Allen Tate's *Poems 1928–31* appeared, followed by Crane's *Collected Poems* and William Carlos Williams' *Collected Poems 1921–31*. In 1934–35, Pound, Eliot, Wallace Stevens, and Marianne Moore were all readying new books.

This is the comparatively immediate background of Schwartz's first poetry. Of his own generation (Randall Jarrell, John Berryman, Theodore Roethke, Robert Lowell), he was the first to publish a book. In spite of his brilliant performance and the very high regard in which he was subsequently held by those whom he respected (Wallace Stevens for example, in a letter to Elder Olsen, May 8,1955, observed, "Schwartz seems to me to be the most gifted of all the younger men" [*Letters* 875]), his reputation did not flourish.

His first book, *In Dreams Begin Responsibilities*, contains a short story by the same name, a long poem, "Coriolanus and His Mother: The Dream of One Performance," a set of eleven poems titled "The Repetitive Heart" with the subtitle "Eleven Poems in Imitation of the Fugue Form," twenty-four separate lyric poems, and a verse drama, "Dr. Bergen's Belief." As heterogeneous a grouping as possible, this is nevertheless bound together in theme and style.

One of Schwartz's greatest achievements is his ability to convey the sense of being, the "withness" not of the "heavy bear" alone but of the total self in the world. The one never exists without the other—the self *and* the world—no more for Schwartz than for Martin Heidegger. But, of course, where Heidegger discusses, Schwartz shares. This he does better than any other poet of his generation and his convolutions of self-consciousness, his obsessive concern with origin and identity work to feed everything in as grist for this same mill. Schwartz stopped, it seems, at the fact of consciousness.

In the musical comedy *Man from La Mancha,* there is a scene where Don Quixote finally must meet The Great Enchanter in combat. His opponent enters, thrusts up his shield and suddenly Quixote is faced with a mirror that is the face of the shield. Other mirrors spring up on other arms all around him. Bewildered, he looks into them and begins to weep. In a way, this is the predicament of Schwartz: not that he is concerned with self, and with himself alone, but that he is concerned with the fact of his own consciousness in the world, what it means, the experience of it physically as well as every other way. For the majority of us this is a "given" from which we go on. Schwartz went on, too, but he returned to this seldom framed, infrequently articulated "given" over and over again, and the wonder of it found expression in everything he wrote.

The focus of his work is long for the time in which he wrote, a time when the distance between the subjective and the objective as presented in art was growing shorter. Journeys into the subconscious, excusably distorted language in nets of ellipses, pages of detail used to describe a second's experience, demented landscapes and fragmented inscapes, identities running into each other like quicksilver, combining, flowing, losing themselves—these are some of the techniques of close focus of which Schwartz does not avail himself. Never for a moment does he vary the medium focal length (the distance between the artist and the subject) with which he seeks to communicate. This is a strength and a limitation, and within it he remains lucid, communicative, and compelling, making use of other means to attain intimacy. An important means is this awareness of self, stated and restated as a theme. Also, he is continuously explicit about ordinarily private matters; unmasking is an important tool. In addition, the intimacy is gained by another factor entirely, but one which hinges on what has just been said. It is the time factor.

Herbert Creekmore of New Directions Press invited comments on Schwartz's work from a number of writers. Robert Warshaw says that Schwartz "seems to me one of the very few American writers who . . . set down the true qualities of modern experience," and John Crowe Ransom writes that Schwartz demonstrated "extreme intelligence in his probings of the *modern world*." Wallace Stevens says that Schwartz is interested in things "as they are seen from the point of view of the understanding of *recent years*." Mark Van Doren refers to Schwartz's stories as having a flavor "which suits perfectly with the fact that the author lives . . . wholly *in our* time" (quoted with permission of James Laughlin, publisher of New Directions Press). Thus, those who write about Schwartz's work usually find themselves commenting on his contemporaneity, largely because of the sense of intimacy. It is not his style, the tools he uses, that are so modern. It is that he writes from a fix on the fact of Being, on, quite often, "Being" itself. Using the middle focus, late nineteenth century, early twentieth, he forces this fact into the reader's awareness, decorating it with a fine set of readings from his cultural heroes. This contributes no more, quite often, than decoration, because what he is doing, although it looks like explanation, is really illumination. When this fact becomes the main theme, the stock of additional insight and reference becomes as externalized as a Matisse painting.

Throughout *In Dreams Begin Responsibilities* Schwartz makes no bones about his cultural forebears. In various contexts he evokes the spirits of Socrates, Marx, Freud, Beethoven, Mozart, and Picasso, and makes other references to Rilke, Joyce, Eliot, Yeats, Shakespeare, Baudelaire, Hölderlin, and Vivaldi. His personal library at the time of his death consisted of 144 books of which the important ones—only a very few—are wildly annotated. His copy of *Ulysses* looks like the Talmud, a small amount of text lost in a scribble of commentary. His Rilke—*Duino Elegies*—is not far behind in the accumulation of marginalia.

All of these matters act as clues to Schwartz's sense of reality and form an approach to his style. The style is not expressionistic; it is not "atonal"; it is not process-ridden. Others wrote, before and after Schwartz, who do make this new sound. Long after Rimbaud, writers all the way to John Ashbery have shown how a closer-focused sense of process can be embodied in a fresh style. Nevertheless, although Schwartz's early poems seem to form on the level indicated, their freshness as American literature is undeniable.

A frequently anthologized poem, "In the Naked Bed, in Plato's Cave," develops an exciting juxtaposition of the Platonic abstraction and the immediacy of physical being, the one heightening the other by contrast. This is intensely expressed in the very first line, which is also the title of the poem. The phrase "the naked bed" brings to mind the last line of the last lyric in this book, "Sonnet: O City, City": "When in the white bed all things are made" (138). There is possibly no more pointed, skeletally powerful, sexual vector than is provided by the application of the adjective "naked" to "bed." The essence of all physical life is here contained, the cup of earthy well-being, of unsophisticated physical and mental consciousness could be shared no more effectively.

This is abruptly followed by the phrase "in Plato's cave." There are ways in which Schwartz's poetry, or everyone's for that matter, delivers ideas. Either the idea is expressed in abstract terms extraneous to whatever textural terms but not fully interfused with the rest of the poem, or the idea is no longer abstract but has become absorbed into the poetic context of itself. This phrase, "in Plato's cave," is an example of the second method—the introduction of "Plato" produces the abstraction, the use of Plato's famous figure of the cave *as if* it is not an illustrative figure but a real cave. This is a brilliant way to make the ideal real, or, better said, to help the reader share with Schwartz the process of sophisticating brutal and innocent physical life by adding to it the complexities of mind. Richard Blackmur might have called this "violation of sensibility by idea." Part of the reader shock occurs at the time the line is finished—the realization that this warm "be-in" is open to complexities of interpretation that sum up to the possibility that what is known in the substantial bed is far from substantial, is, in fact, only an imitation of the "real" reality. At last this, in turn, adds up to the additional stab of realization that this is the young man's condition in the poem, that experience must always be this combination of concrete and abstract.

The experience of lying in bed in the early morning awake, alone, and aware is instantaneously shared. The second line, "Reflected headlights slowly slid the wall" (134), heightens the effect of Plato's metaphor. The idea of reflection brings in the whole set of associations linked with "imitation." The introduction of moving lights (headlights) reminds one of the shadows on the cave wall cast by figures moving in front of the light shed by the fire at the back of the cave. At the same time the words act on the real level so that the reader recognizes the experience of seeing the strange sliding shapes of reflected lights on the walls of the bedroom at night and hearing odd knocks inside and outside the house—"Carpenters hammered under the shaded window" (134). He hears the milkman, goes to the window, finds the sight of the sky too much, and goes back to bed. The sky here, in obedience to the full effect of the metaphor, is the static reality of forms posited by Plato, the true reality. A person glimpses this only, can not achieve it for long. So, back to bed and to sleep. Another, additional, association occurs: the street and buildings are also outside the cave. Does "capital" suggest dome?

Then follows a description of the experience that Schwartz found most meaningful, most wonderful—the awakening in the morning. The morning, for Schwartz, is always renewal, the unfolding of fresh consciousness, the beginning all over again of the miracle of living.

> Morning, softly
> Melting the air, lifted the half-covered chair
> From underseas, kindled the looking-glass,
> Distinguished the dresser and the white wall. (134)

At the end, one is reminded of the beginning. The phrase "Plato's cave" carries still another connotation. One feels the vulnerability, the touching limitation of a man as he wakes in Plato's cave—this metaphor connected with one of the great attempts to understand the world and an attempt that makes limitation rather than conquest. He awakens,

> Perplexed, still wet
> With sleep, affectionate, hungry and cold. So, so,
> O son of man, the ignorant night, the travail
> Of early morning, the mystery of beginning
> Again and again,
> while History is unforgiven. (134)

The end returns the reader to an abstraction, the capitalized word, "History," clear, empty, abstract, as earlier in the poem in his reference to the night he had written "The winter sky's pure capital." This is the capital, the abstraction "History," which is "unforgiven," which implies that it is irremediable and unredeemable, that the waking to choice in many ways is illusion.

In an age of informality, the formality of the language in this poem is striking. Joyce spent a book describing the experience of a sleeping and waking man, and the smelting of new words came raw and smoking into congealing syntax and thence to the reader. None of this occurs in Schwartz's work. The syntax is the syntax we know—not even the inversions that have become so interesting and, in many cases, so successful. Thus the focus remains at a distance. Although it is about the revelation of awakening in the morning, although it is a very personal experience that is being related, the reality exhibited is Cartesian. The room is there—outside of Schwartz as are the horses, the street lamps, and the buildings. It is a world with which we are familiar; it is the world at a middle focus, split (healthily?) at some point into the objective and the subjective. The language imputes objectivity. So far as his style goes, for Schwartz there is intelligent knower on the one side and the intelligible world on the other. This is one of the assumptions back of the conforming syntax, the slowness and prosiness of the line. The assets are clarity and rationality in these early poems. And no wonder—his style is dealing with the subject matter for which it was designed, with the rational, cultural buttressing furnished by Schwartz's cultural heroes. In his later work, when his fundamental subject, the self in its consciousness from moment to moment, calls for greater concentration and wider range, his style, seeking to embrace the irrational within this rational frame, can only diffuse and draw on generality, repetition, and ritual. Techniques that require a much closer focus do not seem available to him. In short, one is never taken into the confidence of his total response, only left distrusted on the doorstep of a stylistically conventional edifice. A remarkable poetry was, nevertheless, accomplished within this limitation.

Another fine poem, "The Ballad of the Children of the Czar," was first published in *The Partisan Review*; it marks one of his earliest attempts in the simple flat style "to declare," as he writes in his preface to *Genesis*, "the miraculous character of daily life and ordinary speech" (ix). It is a poem of eighty-two lines divided into six sections and written in unrhymed couplets. The first section introduces the bouncing ball, Schwartz's symbol for novelty in reality, the uncontrollable factor, careless destiny—the same bouncing ball to which and from which people turn for solace in the opening poem of "The Repetitive Heart":

> The children of the Czar
> Played with a bouncing ball
>
> In the May morning, in the Czar's garden,
> Tossing it back and forth. (113)

The use of the children of the Czar in their apparent security rings an ominous note; their destiny is known. Also the background of the poet is introduced in section two, which stays in the same time period but skips to America:

> While I ate a baked potato
> Six thousand miles apart,
>
> In Brooklyn, in 1916,
> Aged two, irrational.
> . . . .
> O Nicholas! Alas! Alas!

> My grandfather coughed in your army,
> . . . .
> Then left for America
> To become a king himself. (115–16)

The shift shows the far distant effects of ancestry in the process of reaching across the globe (another ball) to determine the life of the poet. Part III makes this explicit in the quite simple style.

> I am my father's father,
> You are your children's guilt. (114)

In this poem the theme of freedom of will is considered from several different perspectives and effectively dramatized in apparently simple factual statements that are neither factual nor simple.

> The child is Aeneas again;

> Troy is in the nursery,
> The rocking horse is on fire. (114)

Aeneas defended Troy in innocence, never suspecting that the gift of the horse would be his undoing and would determine his destiny. The tenor of this metaphor is the child, the young author accepting the gift of himself from his father innocently, unaware of the degree to which his life is determined. The quiet statements continue to a climactic close.

The next section goes back to the doomed brother and sister, children of the Czar, who are bouncing "The bounding, unbroken ball," "unbroken" carrying the connotation of the far-reaching and inviolable connection between these children and their destiny and the poet and *his*. The connection is the illusion of free will that masked both sets of determined lives and, as the poet writes in Part V, "Makes no will glad." But although the children are innocent since they believe, without thinking, that *they* are controlling the ball, they are, at the same time, *not* innocent, since

> They are their father's fathers,
> The past is inevitable. (115)

They inherit from, thus reconstitute, remoter ancestors. This is a theme that permeates all of Schwartz's work. It permeated his life as well; he often reviewed the smallest incidents in his life, going over his childhood with a fine comb. This compulsion is one of the links in the chain that keeps him from sounding more modern. What he searched for was meaning, hidden meaning, and he found that

> Troy is in the nursery
> The rocking horse is on fire.

In the end, he told a friend that he was for "The Good, the True and the Beautiful," behind which is the insistence on the rational and therefore on the meaningful. In an age of irrational man, this compulsion to find rational meaning results in an old sound. It is the sound of culture as we have known it in the past. Although the topics are modern and presentation fine, some of the poems lack the breathtaking quality of contemporary experience that poems by lesser poets have. This deficiency may not seem possible in a poet of whom the hear and the now is a major theme, but, on the level of philosophic and literary style, it is the case.

Section six, the final part of the poem, brings all of the children together in the similarity of their experience. If they knew what was happening to them as the poet now, at the time of the writing knows, they would all have grown up at the same moment and through the same experience. The poet, aged two, is in his highchair, playing with his baked potato, his "buttered world," and this is also a ball that can bounce (and smash!), for it falls off his plate onto the floor, and he begins to cry. At the same time the poet has a vision:

> And I see the ball roll under
> The iron gate which is locked.
>
> Sister is screaming, brother is howling,
> The ball has evaded their will.
> . . . .
> And is under the garden wall.
> I am overtaken by terror
>
> Thinking of my father's fathers,
> And of my own will. (116)

This is wonderfully controlled expression of intense terror. The diction is very like the simple statements that comprise Stevens' "The Man with the

Blue Guitar." The important communication is through the accumulation of such statements. There are parts like this in other Schwartz poems, but few of the poems are pitched all the way through on the level of this deadly quietude.

As for more direct influence on his poetry, there is little doubt that Yeats, Eliot, and Auden played the major roles, while Rilke and Joyce were his later preoccupations. And Shakespeare was always present, much more so in Schwartz's writings than in that of any of his contemporaries. It is not hard to hear the Audenesque voice—" 'He is the one you do not know, my dear' " (88), "Moving together through time to all good" (104); or the Eliot influence, "Which I shall suffer and act again" (94), " 'Little they get. Being nor good nor evil, / Except as driven, they desire merely / A bit of salt for cucumbers in May, / A movie once a week, a game to play' " (43); or Yeats both in rhetoric and in rhythm, "And that strange man on the cross" (121) and "Lest their infinite play / And their desires be / Shadow and mockery" (121). Schwartz makes use of the trimeter in the fashion of Yeats but with a harder surface of both rhetoric and idea that more closely resembles early poems by Auden. Often both influences reign simultaneously.

Several of the lyrics, which include the Auden and Yeats influence, are spare, tight, and of considerable distinction. They possess a pared-down quality never equaled in the later poems, which are softer and comparatively relaxed. Taken in their order of appearance in Schwartz's first volume, they begin with the beautiful "Socrates' Ghost Must Haunt Me Now." This poem is a compendium of Schwartz's main themes set in a tetrameter that is speeded up by introductory trochees and an occasional extra syllable. The tone is exultant and hopeful, based on the fact that Socrates' message is "I do not know I do not know" (118). The poet faces him with his situation, which Socrates describes in six lines before he gives his final comment. The reader will recall the situation, that humankind has only the illusion of freedom and this is based in the "whims of appetite," that he or she is small and limited—"The butterfly caged in electric light," and also subject to illusion, "Love is not love, it is a child / Sucking his thumb and biting his lip" (118).

No more direct or pointed statement of Schwartz's concern with a deterministic past in a violent present, both knit by self or selfhood, can be found in his work than in the brief, Audenesque "By Circumstances Fed." This is quoted in full since it is a statement of Schwartz's deepest preoccupation—his own being—set against the themes just stated so that these are the frame or background:

By circumstances fed
Which divide attention
Among so many dead,
Even in the blooming sun,
For this is not ended,
Never having begun,
And this is attended
By a fire-like power,
Converting every feature
Into its own nature,
As, once in the drugstore,
Between the salves and ointments
I suddenly saw, so strange there,
Amid the sand and soda,
Rich in all appointments,
My own face in the mirror. (123)

The first ten lines are admirably condensed with just two stresses in each line. When the poet moves into the presentation of the concrete experience, he requires more room in the line; he expands, as if it takes more words, more qualifications to present the physical world than to present ideas. The stretching, paradoxically, speeds the lines rather than relaxes them, an effect of the extra syllable and the feminine ending of each line. And when, in his later poetry, Schwartz tries to describe the combination—the celebration of the physical world as it is transcended in a reaching toward the metaphysical—he attempts a fusion of the concrete and abstract via feeling, and the poetic line expands further, just like a solid being turned into a gas. It occupies more space but becomes more tenuous.

The last line of "By Circumstances Fed" is the subject of which the first-line phrase, headed by an understood "is," is the predicate. Thus its reference is to "my own face in the mirror / By circumstances fed." The first three lines refer, of course, to the theme of origins, with the denial of free will. Added to this the fourth line introduces the blazing present in "the blooming sun" and the feeling of continuous process that is often conveyed in Schwartz's poetry by the use of such words as "endless" and "inexhaustible" and also by the word "amid," which is used in many of his poems. "Amid" emphasizes the fullness or plentitude of things, the fact of inescapable and endless context. In addition, Schwartz adds that all this is "attended by a fire-like power" that converts everything to its own nature.

This is Schwartz's portrayal of the self, both the physical self ("time is the fire in which we burn") and the psyche. Now, it is not merely that he characterizes the self as converting everything to its own nature, but it is the additional preoccupation with his own face that begins to hint at Narcissistic emphasis. Finally, in the adjective "strange," both the shock at the fact of consciousness and the attempt to realize selfhood or identity are fully communicated.

"Saint, Revolutionist" is written in a Yeatsian trimeter; it is, in fact, more Yeats than Schwartz, especially the last two stanzas. Also, Yeats took from Blake and so does Schwartz—"Neither in hell nor heaven / Is the answer given" (121). In this poem Schwartz pauses to ruminate. It is perhaps natural that the meditative note should be picked up from Yeats, who was such a master of it that even the trimeter is able to sustain it. The pause is real, the mediation true, for Schwartz is considering a matter that is, in one sense, alien to his own nature. Although he will make immeasurable sacrifice in asserting the sovereignty of poetry and in meeting the expense of being a poet, he is never capable of the abnegation of the saint or revolutionist. In him, self is always assertive. Yet his own sacrifice led him to consider the nature of the total sacrifice made by a saint or a revolutionist. It is a problem that once nonplussed Kenneth Burke, who felt that there is something drastically wrong about the fact that when we recommend something most highly we say either that people are devoting their lives to it or that they are dying for it. Schwartz is concerned with the motivation of the saint or the revolutionist who dies for the cause. He concludes that hell or heaven are both "servant's pay," and that these are not the concerns of the saint or the revolutionist. They must exist "where no will can descend," because

> they wish to know
> How far the will can go,
> Lest their infinite play
> And their desires be
> Shadow and mockery. (121)

Schwartz has taken the matter from transcendental arenas and uncovered its fundamental necessity to make significance of life. This is the will of the saint and the revolutionist and set beyond opposing wills. It is, of course, the will of the poet, too.

Will is one matter, but free will is another. The person who has free will is the one who *can* make a choice. He is the one who unhesitatingly makes decisions that involve other lives, the one who "is willing" to act. Schwartz addresses a poem to him—"For the One Who Would Take Man's Life in His Hands." This, too, carries overtones from Yeats, but it is a far better poem than "Saint, Revolutionist." The iambic tetrameter, occasionally rushed along by an introductory trochee, has been used by Yeats, as has the mode of questioning and answering by the personae in the poem. And Yeats's poetry, more than once, concerned itself with the differences between the activist life and the quietist life, opposing terms in Schwartz's poem as well.

Schwartz begins by citing circumstances in life or literature that demonstrate a fundamental irony:

> Tiger Christ unsheathed his sword,
> Threw it down, became a lamb.
> Swift spat upon the species, but
> Took two women to his heart.
> Samson who was strong as death
> Paid his strength to kiss a slut. (120)

The stanza thus gives examples of battlers who contradict their nature by loving, who are, indeed, betrayed by love. The second stanza, explicit about the irony, reveals the contradiction clearly in explaining why these men reached out to women.

> When all are killed, you are alone,
> A vacuum comes where hate has fed.
> . . . .
> Love is the tact of every good,
> The only warmth, the only peace. (120)

If the soldier is the activist and if Schwartz is dealing in contradiction here, then, of course, the lover is the quietest. And the lover is not occupied with the domination of other people's lives. Soldier or lover, the man who makes a choice is involved in a universe filled with contradiction. Identifying with his mask, Socrates, Schwartz adds,

> "What have I said?" asked Socrates,
> "Affirmed extremes, cried yes and no,

Taken all parts, denied myself,
Praised the caress, extolled the blow,
Soldier and lover quite deranged
Until their motions are exchanged." (120)

He answers with a caution "For the One Who Would Take Man's Life in His Hands,"

"What can any actor know?
The contradiction in every act,
The infinite task of the human heart." (120)

This is one of Schwartz's earliest explicit statements of his concern with the fact of contradiction. His own heart as time passed set itself this "infinite task" and, in the effort, his later poetry loosened, expanded. Never again was Schwartz able to give profound expression such economy as in these early poems.

"Coriolanus and His Mother"

Although deservedly famous, the short story "In Dreams Begin Responsibilities," which both names and begins Schwartz's first book, must be glossed here, since it is not poetry, with the remark that the author's device, in which he pictures himself dreaming that he is watching a performance, is used in other of his works as well. It forms, in fact, the basic structure of the second piece in the book, "Coriolanus and His Mother: The Dream of One Performance."

This presents the author's dream of himself witnessing Shakespeare's play *Coriolanus*. Not only is he part of the audience, but also a commentator between the acts. The poem is divided into five acts written in blank verse; these note the action of *Coriolanus* and comment on it. In addition, five prose pieces are included, one between each act. Thus the "poem" is an amalgam of prose and poetry, another method used more than once by Schwartz in later works. As the plot of the enacted *Coriolanus* is unrolled, it is also evaluated through comments of the author attending the dream performance and by the ghosts of great men of the past who are at his side. Thus, we are treated by Schwartz, the author, to an art work projecting Schwartz, the subject, and the five "influences" watching the Shakespearean drama of *Coriolanus*. The device marks the tremendous self-conscious-

ness of this poet. It signals, as well, an urban intellectual sophisticatio
that begins in self-awareness.

Coriolanus has been considered a play about either a limited militar
mind (Bacon 332 ff) or an arrogant spoiled aristocrat who got his just desert
(Ralli 321 ff). These are nineteenth-century attitudes; a later analysis see
the character Coriolanus as Narcissus, and a still later one shows him as
vehicle for his mother's ambitions. Although outwardly martial, his filia
compliance is a weakness that eventually causes his death. In the Schwart
poem, Coriolanus is in part presented as the victim of an unresolved Oedi
pal complex. His relationship to Aufidius, to whom he ran from Rome
and his relationship with his wife point to the powerful Oedipal inculca
tion. The relationship of mother and son has far-reaching results.

Coriolanus' nature is such that he either breaks or does not break; h
never bends. When the core of an action involves personal integrity versu
the rules of society and an uncompromising protagonist who undergoe
too great a stress, as is the case here, then the protagonist breaks. Fo
Coriolanus, it is initially a question of equating himself with the scum o
humanity he despises or of maintaining an impregnable image. It might b
said those who live by the image die by the image. Coriolanus, insisting o
unrealistic values and perpetrating like a crime the impossible self-image
brings about his own death.

First, however, the question: Why choose Coriolanus rather than som
other protagonist? Can one, in any fashion, equate Schwartz's situatio
with that of Coriolanus? An initial comparison reveals glaring resemblances
For one thing, the Roman is set apart. Although an aristocrat, which i
itself separates him from the general populace, he holds himself aloof from
his own class. Today we might say that he is alienated. In response to hi
need for perfection of personal integrity—his image—he can conform a
no point for the sake of conforming. The assertion of his individuality
which he considers noble, takes precedence over all considerations. Being
alienated, he is alone. Being nonconformist, he is ostracized. Being pub
licly arrogant, he is exiled and, in Rome, narrowly escapes with his life a
the beginning of the play.

Schwartz also started out with several counts against him. He was
Jew; he was an intellectual; he was an artist. This was more than sufficien
to alienate him. In addition, he was excessively sensitive and distrustful. I
was not merely personal meaning he sought; it was a long-term cultura
identity, and he seems to have looked everywhere except in his own Jewisl
heritage. Yet this effort was limited by his unwillingness to submit to

tradition or his inability to find one in which he felt at home. It could be said that he suffered from a frustrated sense of history. And so, it is not surprising that he enlists the participating comments of Aristotle, Socrates, Marx, Beethoven, and Freud to buttress his view of Coriolanus. These men are names, insights, ideas, ideals to Schwartz; they are the color of his sensibility, the size and sharpness of his intellect.

Schwartz was a philosophy major in college, although he became a teacher of literature. Ideas are important to him, and he has as strong a passion for ideas as for poetry. However, he seldom absorbs them into his poetry: ideas are presented in their own substance and appear in the flow of his poetic work as pebbles in a stream. Often they are beautiful, hard, and clear, but just as frequently they block the flow. Schwartz is interested in the perspectives contributed by his culture heroes; these men are important influences; they help to forge the modern consciousness of Delmore Schwartz. If one is to watch the destiny of this consciousness, one should accept their active role in its formation.

Schwartz dramatizes the importance of these influences, showing them as spectators at the play. He sees himself listening to their conversation, records it carefully. Poetry and prose alternate; blank verse establishes the background situation:

> Theatre, the place to stare, rustles of the program,
> Many have come, are being seated. The house
> Is full, the audience is distinguished,
> And in a box seat sit five ghosts, and one,
> A boy with a guttural voice full of emotion.
> The lights dim, half-darkness now accents
> The footlights' glitter before the curtain. The curtain
> Rises on the heart of man. (23)

Thus, Schwartz begins the account of Shakespeare's play. First, Brutus incites the mob, then Menenius, the "canny patrician" (24), addresses the people of Rome. His is the good-fellow attitude in contradistinction to that of Coriolanus, who scorns the populace. Marcius (Coriolanus) has a fine foil in Menenius: the rigid as opposed to the forgiving; the Platonic as opposed to the Aristotelian; the individual as opposed to the many. The antithesis can continue indefinitely: the former (Coriolanus type) standing with the rationalist against the empiricist; the defensive against the outgoing; form as against content; order as against expression; stability against temperament. The former is apt to be cold, calculating, defensive, selfish, standoffish—all except where the value system of the image dictates the opposite stance, charity, generosity, and warmth. The negative responses on the "Menenius" side, characteristics such as sloppiness, lack of selectivity, dirt, and disorder are manifested in the masses in *Coriolanus*.

One could say that Schwartz, who was a wonderfully intelligent and richly gifted man, an intellectual aristocrat seeking the development of complex identity and knowing that his growth could not continue within the confines of negation and aristocratic rejection and having no orthodoxy into which he could fit, with more than a touch of masochism as well as ambition, reached out for a means of growth. The essential method was the attempt to enfold all that at first repelled his geometric abstraction making, aristocratic faculties. He sought to incorporate everything. It is as if Coriolanus, regardless of his unutterable loathing, put out his beautiful arms to clasp to his broad and perfect bosom all the blotched, dirty, and imperfect noggins of the slums of Rome. If you can't fight 'em, join 'em, or "nothing can be sole or whole / That has not been rent" (Yeats 255).

Thus, at the beginning of the poem Marcius is saved from the mob by the newsboys shouting that war is declared, and one great ghost, Marx, makes the first comment: " 'So by death's poverty is poverty escaped, / . . . War being the state's good health' " (26). Then Brutus and a confederate discuss Marcius as " 'so proud' " (27) and " 'insane, alone in his fantasy. / . . . We are not safe until he's cast aside' " (27). Marcius is recognized as dangerous. The scene shifts to the sitting room, where Marcius' mother is introduced. She baldly avows that she would have preferred Marcius to have been her husband rather than her son, shifting the nature of his service to her just sufficiently to introduce the forbidden nature of her relationship with Marcius. One might say that she is conscious of this since she makes the open avowal, " 'Were he my husband as he is my son, / This would delight me O much more' " (28) and then at the end of her speech she refers to him as " 'my son, my spear' " (28).

Here even the strongest stomach must turn, for, against the psyche of this woman, a most repulsive indictment must be made. As Schwartz sees it, and he probably sees it correctly judging from the authenticity of his presentation, Marcius' mother, in calling her son her spear, is not merely saying that he exists to act out her aggressions in society; any soldier who would fight to defend her prerogatives could do that and there would be no personal relationship at all. But this is the case of a mother and son, and her symbol is explicit and truthful. This domineering, aggressive, selfish woman would like to implement these qualities (subconsciously sexually) and would use her son for that purpose. It may be questionable taste to mention this, but it is important to realize in fullest the underlying disdain on the part of the mother for the boy in the man and the man in the boy. Awareness of such a psychically crippling relationship helps one understand the symbols as they are meant to be understood. What could be more contemptuous, more exploiting, more injurious to a growing human soul than the subtle purposes that, deep underneath, guided the hard upbringing of poor Marcius? The delicate psyche was subjected to such reductive treatment that only the deepest feelings of unworthiness could have resulted, and only the strongest assertion of worth could counteract this. The assertion in Coriolanus is insanely strong, and no wonder.

Schwartz may not have had these conjectures in mind at the starting point. It is certain, however, that he moved in this direction during the time of writing, and he realized, more than most of us, to what depths one must reach for an understanding of motivation. He has Freud comment on this scene between Marcius' mother and his wife:

> This is the origin, this, this is the place
> Mother in love with son, and son with her,
> And his aloneness in the womb began. . . . (28)

But Freud says little more of consequence, although when, historically, he said this for the first time, it *was*, of course, of considerable consequence. Marx hastens with the counterstatement that society shaped Marcius, not his relationship with his mother. In the 1930s, a young man watched Marx on his way out the back door and Freud coming in the front. It is most understandable that Schwartz wishes to present these as influences and let them wrangle out the problems.

Marcius, alone, wins the battle. He alone enters the enemy walls, is closed in, comes out again, and calls his men forward to victory. "Hating all men, he was fulfilled in war" (30). Yet *this*, the hate element, is only part of a whole. Later in exile from Rome, Marcius headed directly for his major foe, Aufidius—"for hate, / Love, and desire concentrate their blaze" (31). One must not lose sight of the love and the desire.

Marcius' oscillation between enormous gratification at the idolatry offered him on his return to Rome and the shame he feels at having this gratification revealed causes him to feign modesty and to refuse the money offered him. A man who wants fame shows that he places great faith in his fellow men, in their thought and being. No amount of arrogance can hide the fact that if others did not matter, fame and praise would not matter. He refuses the money:

> And the refusal may dress his nakedness,
> His sheer delight, his shame to be delighted. . . . (32)

The all-devouring, all-encompassing vision of himself cannot accept the material reward. Such an acceptance would demean by implication the pure autonomy, the Godhead, of his vision. The rage at the original frustrations and deprivations in his early life, this rage that afterward was displaced from the mother to this rest of humankind, could be quieted, if at all, by the people giving back to Marcius his exact vision of himself, and they could do this simply by according him their fullest agreement. If all of nature agreed with him (the condition of the infant or of God), then he achieved a simulacrum of the former, gingerbreaded with feelings of being the latter.

There is no point in adding detail. The purpose here is to try to understand the mechanics of Schwartz's identification with Coriolanus, his *use* of the poem. In some places the pat identification falls short; in many it is illuminating. It is old hat that the poet as maker shares a kind of creativity with God, that he must reject stereotype and be cautious about rendering unto Caesar. It is easy to see how a young poet, insistent on cleansing his work of dead matter, superfluities, the lifeless and automatic, must drive for identification with Coriolanus' assertion of integrity. Only the strongest and purest and most continuous defense against compromise holds off the forces of disintegration. No victory must rely more on the strength of one's nobility than the victory of the poet.

It is not necessary to extend the parallel between Marcius and the poet beyond the facts that Schwartz had no father available as he was growing up. He was brought up by his mother and his aunt; the aunt was the warm and true mother, yet she was—and no way to get around it—only the aunt. It is not strange that the young man in one way or another had to become his mother's revenge on her husband, who had rejected both of them. Mr. Schwartz was a hardheaded businessman; the open rebellion of the son shows in the young poet's rejection of every value for which his father stood. He rejected business; he rejected power; and he rejected his father's picture of reality. Delving beneath all of these, he chose his own weapons, and the picture one sees of this courageous poet beleaguered, in a world of money, fighting with only words and ego-assertion, is not too different from the picture of Marcius.

In the ensuing action, although Marcius rejects the money and applause with anger, he accepts, blushing and moved, the addition to his name— Coriolanus. From now on he is called Caius Marcius Coriolanus. One recalls the possibility of traumatic effect, and certainly the importance, of the oddness of the name of Delmore Schwartz. Literary evidence of this is shown in the naming of the "I" in the autobiographical poem, *Genesis*, the name being Hershey Green, and in the verse play, *Shenandoah*, which is about the naming of an infant boy who was finally given the name "Shenandoah" added to his family name of "Fish." Naming has indeed a more than superficial or accidental import here. From aboriginal rituals of naming to Locke's theory of meaning, the nature of naming has been connected with creating—"In the beginning was the Word." There is a possible equation between the singularity of Delmore Schwartz's name and the fact that a special name was also given to Caius Marcius.

The identification of author and character becomes explicit in the last stanza of the first section. As the music ceases,

> Amazed as never before, myself I see
> Enter between the curtain's folds, appear
> As many titter and some clap hands in glee,
> . . . .
> From the box-seat I see myself on show. (33)

This is the introduction to the first of the five prose passages titled "Between the Acts." The first one is subtitled "Pleasure." Here the two levels, author and projection of author watching the play, meld. One knows that one is being spoken to directly; one is not listening merely to a description of a play. This is direct address by the author to the reader and, at the same time, an address by the young man in the audience who has somewhat clownishly stepped up to the stage and parted the curtains. Thus, the reader becomes a double audience: the real-world reader and also the one in the audience listening to the young man who has climbed onto the stage. Of course, these are one and the same reader, but a reinforcing dimension of participation has been added.

In a sense Schwartz uses his person as a persona. His persona is candid, flatly honest, while, as author, he so manipulates the tone and the levels through which it operates that special effects are achieved. One of these effects is the tone of the prose passage "Pleasure." Here the flat and the ordinarily sententious becomes sarcastic, ironic, sometimes dramatic and, in an odd way, analytical.

> I come, I said, to be useful and to entertain. What else can one do? Between the acts something must be done to occupy our minds or we become too aware of our great emptiness. It is true, we might converse with one another. But then we would learn again how little all of us have to say to each other. (34)

The tone, at first, seems to be earnest; only the antecedent action, the use of persona makes it suspect. "What else can one do?" One can do many things, so this must be understood as a weighty, philosophical shrug. "Between the acts" carries the implication of "All the world's a stage" and so refers to more than the action of Coriolanus, a heavy-handed irony. The flat, calm statement, "It is true, we might converse with one another," used instead of a shriek, adds measured quality, a note of enforced patience; it is the sound of a broken spring. It is a man who recognizes, really knows, that there is no way out . . . unless it is through art which allows him this wry mode. It is almost the tone of a teacher who is teaching down to a serious but not too bright class. But since he is presumably addressing his peers, the tone also implies that the comments, true as they are, bespeak a situation that is hard to tolerate but unchangeable.

In these early prose pieces are some of the themes found in Schwartz's work to the very end. He asks, "Why be desperate, even quietly?" (36) and then complains:

> Because one end merely leads to another one, one activity to another one, one activity to another in an inexhaustible *endlessness* which is exasperating. . . . (36)

Coriolanus must conquer all to make a mirror that will give him the necessary image. Schwartz must consume all; his ego must incorporate all before he can be complete. That is why the endlessness gags him. He writes here a wonderful paean to pleasure, defining it first as "the intrinsicality of being, each thing and each state taken as final and for itself" (36). After naming all the pleasures he has known directly or vicariously—"the mystery of being called Mrs. for the first time" (36–37)—after this long list of incorporated joys, he says, "And yet, I know, all this is nothing, nothing consoles one, and our problem and pain are still before us" (38). Pleasure is finite; he has said it is not endless; he has pain which he says is "selfish" (38); it is also individual. What is he yearning for when he yearns for this "endlessness" to end? He must attain the same circumstance that Coriolanus must reach. He must, in his unfortunate fashion, conquer all.

But he feels unsure. Act II begins, "Absurd and precarious my presence there" (39), and he is happy to see the curtain rise and to find himself back in his seat in the audience. In other words—and this is only a part of it—he is glad to don the mask of the persona, both to reveal art and to hide behind it. Everyone comes out to see the triumphal march and, finally, the warrior stands "ashamed / To take of their plaudits so much flushing pleasure" (40). Then Schwarz again marks the profound relationship between mother and son. Coriolanus

> descends
> Unto that great primordial circumstance
> Which holds him yet,
> "O Mother, Mother," kneeling,
> Thus he descends to her, "All that I did
> I did for you." (40)

This is commented upon by, oddly enough, "The snub-nosed Freud" (40). Freud was certainly not snub-nosed, but Socrates was. Another mix-up that may be of the same order. In the third prose section, titled "Choose," Schwartz tells the story of Coriolanus' journey away from Rome. He describes Caius Marcius Coriolanus as follows: "He sees his face, his thick lips, curly hair, flaring nostrils, broad forehead. His haunted eyes regard themselves, round lakes full of a kind of sweat" (69). These may be or may not be the lineaments of Coriolanus, but they do add up to a description of Schwartz himself, even to the fact that his "eyes regard themselves," a way of characterizing the kind of poem this is. Was this apparent mistake planned or unconscious? If this were in a novel, speedily composed, one could accept it as error. Not so in poetry. By such means Schwartz melds the influences, that of five great ghosts, to place them in one mind, that of the author, and then he identifies himself with Coriolanus as the evidence shows above.

Cominius recites the public biography of Coriolanus and all his exploits, at which the hero flees the scene "like a puking girl / Upset by joy" (41). This is not the first time Schwartz refers to Coriolanus in disdainful terms as a female. Identification with Coriolanus is one thing, but the use to which the identification is put is another. Schwartz identifies not to vindicate himself or his object of identification but to consume and transcend. His identification is never wholly compassionate, gentle, or kind; it is predatory. He says at the end of the first prose passage:

> Let us continue to gaze upon it. Let us, I say, make a few sharp clear definite observations before we die. Let us judge all things according to the measure of our hearts (otherwise we cannot live). Let us require of ourselves the strength and the power to view our selves and the heart of man *with* disgust. (38)

He does not scruple to tear at himself. Why should he hold back with Coriolanus? This passage contains a credo that Schwartz followed for the rest of his life. In it he makes the crucial statement that, when examined carefully, reveals seeds of destruction. "Let us judge all things according to the measure of our hearts" seems to say that we should temper our judgments with true feeling. But, really, it goes further. First, it says nothing about amelioration; "all things" are to be judged unequivocally, and by what yardstick?—"the measure of *our* hearts," neither more nor less. In other words, let us stand by our own vision of things. A result of this insistence is the rejection of "other minds." But sanity is measured by the degree to which one accepts the fact of other minds.

Cominius continues his speech until he comes to the last war, where he reaches the acme of his praise:

> Again and again
> War after war, the champion in each,
> Until before Corioli his war alone,
> Sole, single, absolute, *per se*, alone
> (Aseity such as is God's alone). . . . (41)

The comment by Freud, directly following, is really concerned with Schwartz; the substance of Schwartz himself is involved, although it is Coriolanus about whom Freud speaks. The revealing statement is:

> "found solitude most sweet,
> Prided himself thereon, and felt contempt
> For all not self-contained as he. . . ." (42)

And Freud adds,

> "The past is always present, present as past,
> It grasps us like Athena by the hair. . . ." (42)

The second prose interlude is titled "Justice." Schwartz tells an old story that was recounted to him as a boy by this father. It is the well-known story of a man, his son, and a pony. They were on a journey and although they started with the man walking and the pony carrying the boy, they were forced by the opinion of each stranger that they met to change their positions. Finally, when the father finds himself and his son carrying the pony on the advice of the last stranger, and they thus become a laughingstock when entering the marketplace, he shoots his son, the pony, and himself. One can see this, perhaps, as the other side of the same coin on which is written, "Let us judge all things according to the measure of our hearts (otherwise we cannot live)."

The interlude ends with a paragraph reminiscent of the short story "In Dreams Begin Responsibilities," where the poet's mother enters, argues long and brutally with the father: "while I wept loudly, watching them, weeping because of the sad end of the story, because they were denouncing each other and because I had been slapped for calling my father a liar" (50). So much for a section headed "Justice." It becomes in context an irony, a reminder of the ever-present power of the past.

In the beginning of Act III, the explicit admission appears at last:

> His story was my story, he was I,
> Myself divided in identity. . . . (51)

There is violence because of Coriolanus' refusal to accommodate the masses. He denounces them with such insistence that even the aristocrats find his extremism distasteful, but this contains the first clear indication of the mode that eventually became Schwartz's:

> "But of all personal animals
> Marcius is most extreme, most radical,
> Discolors with his teeth each element,
> Which gave him being, cooks it, pukes it up,
> So by transforming all, himself to be,
> Though vomiting be all activity,

> Till in the vomit's tint and smell he sees
> His unique essence living as disease." (54)

It should be pointed out that he writes "cooks it," meaning "incorporates it," "digests it," and "pukes it up." To feel the self-contempt here in full the reader might ask himself what he, the reader, is, then, who incorporates it from Schwartz?

The third "Between the Acts" prose interlude is entitled "There Was a City." It is an allegory that sets forth in metaphorical but simpler terms the complex story of the young, creative man born in a finance-power-utility state. The metaphor comparing the development of the capitalistic state with the shipbuilding city places the action at least one remove from realism. It makes possible the combination of poetic density and generalization—eras in the city's history rising and falling in paragraphs, and single sentences assigned to describe major economic shifts. In the synoptic structure one sees the age-old form of the parable and looks for the lesson.

The young man assumes the prerogative of evaluating all kinds of life, rejecting, seemingly without too great an expense, the institutionally prescribed means of obtaining the rewards of the society. A "new and unique center of feeling" (64) is preparing itself in his heart. Because of this creativity, the future of the city is linked with his future. He sets out to sea, but, in order to go forward in directions of his own, he finds it necessary to murder the captain. The piece ends:

> See him! He stands at the prow, observing the glittering possi-
> bilities of the waters as the ship moves forward in time. He is in
> love. I am in love with him! (65)

It seems clear that this is the apology, an attempt to show the other side of Coriolanus/Schwartz. Schwartz has expressed his self-disgust—first through disgust with the human race. Here he expresses his love. It is the hopeful, creative qualities he loves in himself and in Coriolanus. Like Coriolanus, the boy in the story is pure; he insists on his own heart's being the measure of all things. He conforms to none of the acceptable ways. He rejects, finally, all of the society in which he was born, and, like Coriolanus, his exile is self-imposed. He sails away, but with a difference. Coriolanus leaves on his exile with hate; the boy sets forth with love, with hope, and with a creative urge. These are the three qualities with which Schwartz faced his own life: love, hope, and the ability of an artist. This is his picture of himself—the two combined, the boy at the prow of the ship *and* Coriolanus. The difference between the two is not too great. One recalls that the boy, with all his love and hope, starting a voyage to a new life, surrounded by the poetry of Schwartz's allegorical prose, finds "it necessary for him to murder the captain of the ship" in order to set his own course. Again, like Coriolanus, it must be his trip alone. Is he not asserting the necessary sovereignty of the artist whose early arrogance acts as a protection during his green period? Although the murder is metaphorical, it is still murder. It is personal emphasis on the most extreme act of rejection possible. It is without doubt an expression of the intense insistence on purity, on the extreme, therefore, which is to be found in the character of Coriolanus as well.

In Act IV Coriolanus leaves the city, assuring his mother that his letters will be regular, but he is not despairing; he feels himself strong, alone, and "perfect once again" (67). His feeling is extended and justified by the prose interlude immediately following, which is titled "Choose." Choice involves freedom and it is appropriate that the author add his comment on the subject of free will at the juncture where the boy from the shipbuilding city sets sail on his journey and where Marcius Coriolanus starts alone on his exile from Rome.

Then begins the interlude of Coriolanus' wandering when he is a stranger among strange peoples, moving finally to the very opposite pole of his home—his enemy, the ultimate stranger. Note, too, that the motion from one pole to the other is tied irretrievably to rejection between the poles: the rejection of the mores of the shipbuilding city by the boy; Coriolanus' rejection of the Roman populace; and Schwartz's rejection of American materialism.

With insistence on polar choice, Coriolanus runs into trouble. Choice involves freedom of will and this involves morality. Coriolanus never seems to examine the morality of his either-or choices. The little story places this responsibility on him. Coriolanus wanders in the wilderness, and to the reader's mind come other wanderings in the wilderness, all with the same soul-searching, the same spiritual tribulations: the wanderings of Moses and his flock; the loneliness of St. Augustine; the weary and alone Mohammed. Coriolanus, moving angrily and then despairingly through the wilderness, comes at last to a lake; he reaches, in the standard symbolic form, the possibility of spiritual sustenance. He is desolate. Even his mother is against him, "even his sleep betraying him" (69). He has "attainted to the emptiness for which he has striven" (69). This is an early stage on spiritual pilgrimage à la Eliot and St. John of the Cross. On the journey Eliot describes, one empties oneself of worldly things; one neither hopes nor despairs; one waits in a vacuum. Coriolanus, by immense rejection, by insistence on selfhood alone but a selfhood pure and immature, moves into this circumstance as a novitiate *manqué*. He kneels by the lake, regards himself. The reflection with the sky as backdrop or "hat" (69) is Schwartz's face:

> It is the moment of vision and decision. Staring upon that face which is his own, he sees his own life, and the lives rejected and the choices chosen, and the immediacy of anger and pleasure, and the abstracted stare of memory, and the strangeness, to himself, of his own face, the most peculiar of flowers. (69)

As he gazes into the lake, his face is replaced by that of his mother, which blooms and grows into an enormous image. She tells him that he is nothing apart from her; he cannot reject her. His lips, the shape of his head, his "strength, system, urge, habit, complexion, and dress" (70) will be with him wherever he goes and these come from her. She speaks two paragraphs; the first ends:

> "The word of your tongue is mine. Your effort to depart from me is your pain, your evil. I am your mother or Rome. I am Volumnia or Rome." (70)

And then, in the last paragraph, she hands him his strategy for living. She is his, she tells him, but he is his own: " 'lips, face, hair, look, your own, your property. This is your freedom' " (70). His words are his own, although he has taken them from her. She ends her statement with an emphasis on his irreducible individuality, assuring him of his freedom of will:

> "Nothing compels you, no imperative dictates to you, the actuality of your choice is what it is for you, your individuality grasps the uniqueness of each moment. This surpasses me. This is your freedom. Choose!" (70)

Here, again, is the recommended strategy: incorporation. He is to incorporate his mother in order to preserve his own selfhood. This is the first step in a long line of consumption. She promises him that once this is accomplished, he is no longer hers. She is his and he is himself, alone again, and can make his choice. But this is only symbol and gesture. Long before, both Coriolanus and Schwartz had already made the choice that was both irresistible and irremediable.

Part IV, entitled " 'A Goodly House, the Feast Smells Well,' " again brings Coriolanus to the need for decision. Stressing the necessity for a clean-cut choice between opposites, Schwartz shows the curtain rising on a night in which "All's indeterminate except the moon" (71). He shows Marcius Coriolanus in white, faced by two enormous signs painted phosphorescent, one marked "To ANTIUM" (71) and the other "To ROME" (71). The poet points out that the signs are unnatural: "Night over all / Except the rounding moon which dreams of snow, / Unnatural as both signs" (71). In size and color they are unnatural out in the waste, next to each other. But, more central to the theme, the presentation of two extremes to choose from— no possibility of compromise—is also unnatural. Most men find it a necessary, helpful part of maturity to give a little and take a little. But the protagonists of tragedy seldom do; they are the ones who invariably measure all things by their own hearts.

It is true that realization of all the possibilities ensuing from the making of a choice might paralyze one. It is also true that the few do take their lives into their hands, and still fewer do so with significant results. Over and over again, Schwartz refers to Coriolanus as "the absolute" and in this section, moving back to a description of Rome, he writes: "Rome fattens, rid of its poor absolute" (75). The first two words imply complacence, wickedness, and corruption which, of course, is the one pole, while the other is the absolute's purity. Coriolanus, despite damages, is always a man; therefore, so much in the play and in the poem is heroic and noble. That it is a nobility unmodified makes it an absolute; since it is unblessed by humility, some might say, it must also be monstrous.

The end of the section marks the trepidation of Rome when the news breaks that the enemy is coming with Coriolanus at their head. The significant lines here, however, tell how, regardless of his vows to show humility, Coriolanus cannot stop himself from undermining Aufidius. "He gnaws Aufidius with every tooth" (76). This he cannot help, although he has sworn to "move with modesty / And loyalty" (76).

> But the true surd
> Is irreducible. The individual
> Is uncontrollable. To him, to him
> The soldiers draw, forget Aufidius. . . . (76)

The prediction is made that in this fault lies Coriolanus' ultimate downfall.

The existential notion of the irreducibility of the individual is the subject of the last prose interlude, which is titled "He Is a Person." The fact of uniqueness seems somehow for Schwartz an excuse for being "absolute." It is also proof of the ability to choose:

> His uniqueness is obvious, although he resembles other members of his family. His voice has a certain intonation which has never been heard from another man. . . . He is original. (78)

Act V follows on the same theme and is entitled " 'As if a Man Were Author of Himself.' " First, Cominius visits Coriolanus to beg that he spare Rome; then Menenius comes to beg. Both are denied in front of Aufidius. At last Volumnia, his mother, and his wife and child enter. The great scene in which he finally gives in to his mother is described. Socrates in ecstatic tones bears witness to the truth that Coriolanus is the future for his family and Rome:

> "All, all depends on him, on his sole heart.
> He is contingency, it is his will.
> He is the future of time, it is his choice." (84)

In the hysteria of the moment, all ghosts clamoring and Coriolanus and his mother facing each other, Schwartz, the author, intervenes, and asks fearfully who the silent ghost is: " 'Who is that silent one?' I asked in fear, / 'Who is that ghost who has not said one word?' " (86), and he hears the reply:

> "He is the one who saw what you did not!
> He is the one who heard what you did not, . . .
> . . . .
> He is the one you do not know, my dear." (88)

The author, then, is not omniscient. This is what the lines mean, but more than this is implied. What he does not know is dead to him. He is dead to all experience that is not his or, put another way, everything that occurs that he does not experience might just as well never occur or exist as far as his apprehension of life is concerned. It need never have been; it need never be. Thus, one may be said to be largely dead in the first place. One is merely a pinpoint of awareness in the midst of a cosmos of death. This peculiar point of view, this emphasis on the partial, on death, runs through "Coriolanus and His Mother" and much of Schwartz's other work. Death is considered, not surprisingly, over and over again by this poet, but it is always the personal death, the personal limitation in partiality where what is left of the person is only an impermanent victim of further contingency. Coriolanus leads his family safely out, returns to face his death at the hands of Aufidius and his soldiers. As the curtain falls, Aristotle says, " 'Man's will is free, / This man became the man he chose to be!' " (88).

There is no doubt that "Coriolanus and His Mother" is a significant and moving document. That it is a successful poem is doubtful; there are too many formal difficulties. Although the prose interludes fit thematically into the work, they break into the rhythm of the poetic sections. The device of the great ghosts—projecting the actual presence of great men of the past together with their comments into the action of the poem—seems a failure on every count. It slows the action, and worse, the comments add little to the intellectual content. The insights, expressed often awkwardly by the ghosts, are really contained in a subtler and far more effective form in the rest of the poetry. Schwartz gives himself better comments than he gives the spectator ghosts. It is possible that Schwartz was in conflict about using this device but that the ritualistic need he felt for compulsively and publicly counting his intellectual beads, for calling these great ghosts out of their sleep to accept their share of responsibility for the action, was too great. What is presented, therefore, is a poem with all the blueprints and the scaffolding hanging on the outside.

One should note, also, that both the prose sections and the poetry sections are characterized by a frantic juxtaposition of concretes and abstractions. In both sections, general statements pile up and, in their hearts, throbbing with substantiality, the concretes are scattered. And this, for what it is worth, amounts to a breach of decorum. Although one must read large parts of this material to come to any such conclusion, an example or two may help to show the kind of rhetoric referred to here, although not the degree of it or the quantity.

> "Rome fattens, rid of its poor absolute. . . ."

Or

> In the Shakespearean night, the souls of the poor fool and the brave hero . . . shiver and huddle in a nakedness . . . possessing hair, eyes, hands, feet, arms, belly, genitals. . . . (77)

Or

> "The belly-button bleeds! The hero dies!
> Thus will he pay the dialectical price. . . ." (67)

It must be admitted, however, that a tension is created by this style, a feeling of constant motion. One is never permitted to relax into an expectation of either smoother abstract statements or richer concrete materials. Put another way, one can say that both concretes and abstractions are necessary in a work, but that they are often grossly joined.

Liking this is, of course, a matter of taste. There are good reasons to buttress the feeling that, since the piece is short, the condensed plot of Shakespeare's play (the action unrelieved by full portrayal of character) seems composed of unmitigated violence and, therefore, the rephrasing is bombastic. In such a context, the prose interlude can be considered self-indulgent.

One is inclined to agree with this, but "Coriolanus and His Mother" is a narrative, philosophical poem, possibly the only one of its kind in the twentieth century. The virtue lies in the poetry and in the honesty. The choice of Coriolanus as a persona is brilliant, nor is Schwartz ever evasive here. In this work he faces himself in at least three mirrors: the ghosts, the projected image of himself watching the play and partly participating, and the action of the play within the poem, the destiny of Coriolanus so seriously identified with that of the poet himself.

"The Repetitive Heart"

Of the thirty-five poems in *In Dreams Begin Responsibilities*, eleven are in a separate section called "The Repetitive Heart." The subtitle, "Eleven Poems in Imitation of the Fugue Form," raises many questions as to the degree of resemblance between the grouping and the "fugue form." These questions are not easy to answer, in part because the fugue is not a schematic form; it is a texture. One can only bear in mind the outstanding characteristics of a fugue while giving the poetry a reading.

A fugue is composed of a specified number of "voices" or "parts." The words "voices" and "parts" will be used here to refer to the succession in time of articulated sections of the fugue. More significant, a fugue is monothematic, states a single subject. In the course of the fugal exposition, there is a cumulative beginning, the first part or voice followed by the second, etc., until all the voices enter; thus, the theme or subject, as the fugal melody is called, is stated. After the first exposition, the rest is an unpredictable succession of episodes and partial or full expositions.

There are also a number of special devices that may be used. The pattern of the subject may be either reversed or inverted in subsequent statements. The subject may enter, repeated in the second voice before the first is finished (called stretto); the subject may, in later versions in the fugue, be stated slowly (grandeur), or more rapidly (excitement); finally, there may be a change of mode from major to minor or vice versa, keeping the identity of the subject but darkening or brightening the mood. One fact is apparent: although Schwartz's poems contain metrical variation, it is not of main significance in the fugal comparison. The important contrapuntal play, the repetition in the poems, is a matter of theme or idea, and this may be likened to the "subject" of the fugue.

The first of the eleven poems, then, makes the fugal statement that presumably will be the subject repeated by the different voices. Schwartz begins, "All of us always turning away for solace / From the lonely room where the self must be honest" (91). He lists some typical distractions, all based on playing ball in one way or another (Schwartz was a fervent follower of baseball). He mentions billiards, baseball, and football. He writes that this, indeed, is solace, the "Bounding, evasive, caught and uncaught, fumbled," and then he adds that one follows the bouncing ball, "Fingering closely your breast on the left side" (91). This reminds one of the phrase, "self-squeezing heart" from "Coriolanus and His Mother" and the ending of "Dr. Bergen's Belief," "Man destroys his own heart," because at the end of this first brief poem he again refers to the ball, "The bouncing ball you turned from for solace" (91). The full subject of the total fugue, then, seems to be that there is no solace either in the bouncing ball (the concrete distractions) or in solitude (the honest self facing itself). And this is the case only if Schwartz meant the "fugue form" to apply overall to the eleven poems and not to each one in particular.

The second poem seems to answer the demand for solace, even though offering neither distraction nor honesty. Here he addresses, most gently, "Ruth of sweet wind," and asks her to be his solidity, stability, and fidelity:

> Will you perhaps consent to be
> Now that a little while is still
> (Ruth of sweet wind) now that a little while
> My mind's continuing and unreleasing wind

> Touches this single of your flowers, this one only,
> Will you perhaps consent to be
> My many-branchéd, small and dearest tree? (92)

He sees himself as the wind, which is "wild and restless, tired and asleep." He sees her as his small tree, forever rooted. This is a fond masculine idea of the relationship: she immobile, eternally faithful; and he continuously mobile, shifting with impulse, completely free. Attendant on such a notion there is always excessive tenderness and gentleness for the exploited object; this accounts for the ecstatic sweetness of the tone.

> My dear, most dear, so-many-branchéd tree
> My mind's continuing and unreleasing wind
> Touches this single of your flowers, faith in me,
> Wide as the—sky!—accepting as the (air)!
> —Consent, consent, consent to be
> My many-branchéd, small and dearest tree. (92)

What is also involved is the great thankfulness the poet can feel—the poet in whom the burden of distrust becomes more unendurable yearly—in being allowed to place his trust. Even so, she must be his "smallest" tree. She must be diminutive and firmly rooted before she can become even the slightest solace.

The third poem repeats the different kinds of solace, while the overtones of the first are still echoing. Another tune is added to the subject; "All clowns are masked and all *personae* / Flow from choices" (93). Here the poet loses some of the poetry to the habit of philosophizing. Despite Schwartz's ability to present ideas and his high-pressure interest in them, they seldom diminish the poetry. They may often stand out, be unabsorbed by the poetic line, extraneous, in a sense, to the style, but here they do not block the poetry in a large way. In this case, the conjecture about free will does just that. He continues:

> And yet not so! For all are circumstances,
> Given, like a tendency
> To colds or like blonde hair and wealth,
> Or war and peace or gifts for mathematics,
> Fall from the sky, rise from the ground, stick to us
> In time, surround us: Socrates is mortal. (93)

In some way, we are free in a small scope to make choices but in a large way they are determined for us by a chain of causes or by what we call contingency. Interesting comment that falls out of the rhythm and stumbles past the poetry into prose! The rest of the poem does not. Socrates is chosen because he is the great questioner. He, too, is mortal, which means, in this context, that his freedom likewise is curtailed: "he who chooses chooses what is given" (93). The final comment, a filigree around the subject, states, "He who chooses is ignorant of Choice." This is a reference to the common man of action who makes what he believes are choices, and who must, in order to act decisively, be ignorant of the paralyzing fact that he can only choose "what is given." It is apparent that this is the average man of action because he is not choosing anything except love, which means children. It is children who are the choice and the artist does not choose children. Shaw's *Man and Superman* is a reminder of this.

This section of the "fugue" ends: "So full of choices! So full of children! / And the past is immortal, the future is inexhaustible!" (93). The exclamation points reveal an irony because the promise of immortality through children is imperfect, to put it at its best, and with or without children the feeling that the future is inexhaustible is pure delusion. The irony takes the place, at this point, of the subject of "no solace," and so the subject, although advanced through "filigree," is restated in this poem. On the thematic level, the new point made—that contingency rules, that those who think they choose, choose blindly, "And all our choices grasp in Blind Man's Buff" (93)—may be likened to a part of the arbitrarily short or long section of the fugue, following the statement of the subject and adding to it.

Number four sees a metrical speeding up; the poem is written in iambic tetrameter in most cases with an additional syllable to move it faster. The repetition of certain lines such as "time is the fire in which we burn" (94) adds to his message of the wilderness and momentum of the conflagration of living. This is clearly the statement of the subject again; that this is speeded up for excitement is typical of the fugue. The subject, "Distracted from distraction by distraction," as Eliot says in "Burnt Norton" (178), is given to his comment on the "pauper and *rentier*, / The screaming children, the motor car," when he adds "Fugitive about us, running away" (94). They are, in terms of the original statement, turning to the bouncing ball for solace, then from the bouncing ball for solace. Again the note of determination is sounded:

(. . . that time is the fire in which we burn.)

(This is the school in which we learn . . .)
What is the self amid this blaze?
What am I now that I was then
Which I shall suffer and act again. . . . (94)

The poem ends with the justly familiar characterization of the intimate experience of flux:

The great globe reels in the solar fire,
Spinning the trivial and unique away.
(How all things flash! How all things flare!)
What am I now that I was then?
May memory restore again and again
The smallest color of the smallest day:
Time is the school in which we learn,
Time is the fire in which we burn. (95)

A further investigation in the nature of the self-philosophic, in a sense, continues the fugal texture. This is an addendum to the no-solace theme but by implication only. What is revealed in this, the fifth poem, is the apparently contradictory nature of humankind. The acceptance of the problem of generals and particulars is concretized in the opening lines:

Dogs are Shakespearean, children are strangers.
Let Freud and Wordsworth discuss the child,
Angels and Platonists shall judge the dog. . . . (96)

In this statement the dogs are generals and they are to be recognized by ideals (angels) and idealists (Platonists), while the children are particulars, individual psyches, recognized by Freud (sex, nature) and Wordsworth (romantic trust). The use of "Shakespearean" in this case seems to be carried by the connotation of "types," since some of his greatest characters are considered atypical. The first stanza ends with a line combining both children and dogs in the use of "they"—for *they* are strangers; they are "Shakespearean." This is possible since the preceding lines show that both have sensibility—the girl who "understood the wind and rain" and the "dog who moaned, hearing the violins in concert" (96).

An additional connotation of "Shakespearean" is the reminder of the Shakespearean cosmos that is amenable to magic, a place where abstract evil exists, unpredictable events as well as predictable ones, a dark and wild dome of the ineffable over the heads of humans. Schwartz's "Shakespearean" blank verse questions the insights of Freud and Wordsworth, suggests they are limited:

> And you, too, Wordsworth, are children truly
> Clouded with glory, learnéd in dark Nature?
> The dog in humble inquiry along the ground,
> The child who credits dreams and fears the dark,
> Know more and less than you; they know full well
> Nor dream nor childhood answer questions well:
> You too are strangers, children are Shakespearean. (96)

It must also be clear that, allies on the one hand, Freud and Wordsworth are also poles apart in the sense that the basis for Freud's thought is concrete, the family constellation; Wordsworth's feeling about children contains something mystical if not metaphysical. So, a double layer of seeming opposites—the generals and the particulars and within the particular the secular and the mystical—meld in the last line of the stanza that begins, "You too are strangers." Schwartz is working toward the last stanza where he can make this statement include everyone and, in fact, everything. It begins, "Regard the child, regard the animal," and it ends in a final and third connotation from the "Shakespearean," the implication of "personae" as used in the third poem, that "all the world's a stage":

> And we are howling or dancing out our souls
> In beating syllables before the curtain:
> We are Shakespearean, we are strangers. (96)

Thus, in living, the poles of attempted understanding meet. But classification—generals and particulars—fails in the face of this melding into an "inexhaustible future," mortal and unknown. In the end, Schwartz is, of course, speaking of himself and identifying with the audience.

This brings him to a consideration, in the next poem, number six, of the liabilities of his place in the audience, among people. The subject of the fugue has been extended in the discussion of the limitation, as a solace, of intellectual and poetic enterprise in the prior poem. It is further embroidered upon by the combination in us humans of twin needs that appear to cancel each other out: our need for each other and our need to betray each other, even dearest friends by their friends. There is no doubt that Schwartz's own hostility expressed itself in the distrust exhibited in the opening lines:

> Do they whisper behind my back? Do they speak
> Of my clumsiness? Do they laugh at me,
> Mimicking my gestures, retailing my shame? (97)

The stanza continues, bitterly presenting the experience of suspicion, denunciation, and withdrawal: "nor will I once again / . . . Recognize their faces, take their hands" (97). In the long second stanza, characteristically revealing himself and his own faults, he admits that he, too, betrays his friends. "For wit's sake, to amuse, because their being weighed / Too grossly for a time, to be superior" (97). He is, he writes, betraying the old intimacy for the new momentary intimacy. What solace, then, is friendship? "What an unheard-of thing it is, in fine, / To love another and equally be loved!" (97). Schwartz emphasizes the burden of both sadness and joy. This last stanza dissolves into distracted prose:

> I need
> My face unshamed, I need my wit, I cannot
> Denounce them once for all, they cannot
> Turn away. We know our clumsiness,
> Our weakness, our necessities, we cannot
> Forget our pride, our faces, our common love. (98)

Here the form of fugal filigree entangles, is almost lost in the composer's despair. At his ending, the poem drops—but not quite—into what, as a general error, has been somewhat pontifically referred to in the field of criticism as "the fallacy of imitative form."

In poem seven the poet turns to his feelings for solace; after all, the heart perceives in its own way. This is hopeless. In the first line Schwartz writes, "I am to my own heart merely a serf." He calls this state in which the heart assumes control "incredible assumption," making several suitable puns. But the situation is nothing to pun about:

> I climb the sides of buildings just to get
> Merely a gob of gum, all that is left

Of its infatuation of last year.
Being the servant of incredible assumption,
Being to my own heart merely a serf. (99)

In other words, by any other criterion, his activities are all out of proportion so far as the profit that is to be gained when the heart rules. Nothing is less tasteful, useful, desirable than a gob of gum that one will rechew like a cud, but he is made to climb the side of a building to get it. The incongruity of his action reveals the justness of his self-deprecation. But even if he recovers a bit of the old feeling, "one is sick of chewing gum all day"; his reaction is anger, and sleep is the only means of dissipating it. Not always the case, however. Often "sleep too is crowded . . . full of chores impossible and heavy" (99). Among these chores is the carrying of his father's carriage on his back, another reminder of "origins" and the determining power of one's forebears. This recalls the parable in the fourth prose interlude of "Coriolanus and His Mother." When sleep does not palliate, the poet wakes with his anger renewed and finds himself once more on the misery-go-round of

The unfed hope, the unfed animal,
Being the servant of incredible assumption,
Being to my own heart merely a serf. (99)

The statement is the same statement made at the beginning of the poem—the subject of the fugue merely restated in another voice or part and with, perhaps, the curlique of a bit of extra filigree as well. It is only another substantial statement that we move to the bouncing ball for distraction and from it for distraction. One might say that Schopenhauer is the philosophic grandfather of this fugue, but, in a book replete with culture heroes he is never named. There is frequently, in all of us, an unwillingness to betray to public knowledge the earliest and closest, usually familial, influences. One cannot escape realizing that the great show of disclosure put on by the exhibitionist has its function of obfuscation. That which is closest is inevitably hidden, held in reserve, the entire activity of surface frankness being counted on to protect it. This is more often than not the gambit of Schwartz. Much is revealed by it, but one need not lose sight of the full function of the revelation.

Here in poem seven it is becoming clear that "action is suffering, and suffering action" for Schwartz, and, since Eliot was such a powerful influence, the point is appropriately introduced. From this situation there is no recourse unless it is death. But Schwartz continues to consider the possibilities of solace. The fugal statement will be reiterated.

Now comes the cry for help, whatever help can be gotten from Schwartz's only reservoir, the cultural past: "Abraham and Orpheus, be with me now" (100). He has admitted his need for love as well as his need of betraying it. Now in poem eight he cries out because even when his love is given, it is given to the evanescent, the ephemeral. Of both Abraham and Orpheus the very same strange condition, strange requirement, was made in the name of love, as—in the sense of Schwartz's meaning in both poems—is required of us all. Each had to betray his love to death; and, in the name of love, to sustain this sacrifice. Schwartz is not different, nor is anyone else who cares. It is worse, even, than this, for we do not wait for the death of the beloved. Instead, quite often, "love exhausts itself and falls and time goes round" (100). The love itself fades with time and disappears, which is perhaps the saddest thing of all. Thus, love has a shadow as have all substantial things; it is the shadow of death, really a lovely figure. In this shadow Orpheus drowns, and so must we all. The poem ends, "I ask your learnéd presence, I care and fear, / Abraham and Orpheus, be near, be near" (100). And, of course, what solace are these great myths of the past? They, too, drowned "in the shadow all love always bears" (100).

The magnifying glass Schwartz has been using is also a burning glass, and the reader has gained through this poet's terrifying honesty, but he has been scorched as well. The relentless dialectic continues with the ninth poem. In search for solace, one has been driven away from reliance on ordinary distraction (the bouncing ball); on sweet stability (the many-branched tree that proves to be, ultimately, "the very rack and crucifix . . . of winter's wild . . . ice caressing wind"); on freedom of choice (Blind man's Buff); on the security of the present ("Time is the fire in which we burn"); on the ability to understand our contradictory selves (generals and particulars, classification fails); on friendship ("Do they whisper behind my back?"); on freedom of feeling ("I am to my own heart merely a serf"); on love of mortal things that dies even before natural death ("Love love exhausts and time goes round and round"). Next, one looks to the adequacy of solace through the physical self in its life.

Poem number nine, much anthologized, gives consideration to this problem. The theme is in the quotation from Whitehead that precedes it—" 'the withness of the body,' " but this is still an embroidering around the original fugal statement involving the lack of solace. Some might write about the joys of the body; in fact, in one of the interludes in "Coriolanus and His Mother" Schwartz does mention the joys of the athlete. But this poem goes deeper. Even the athlete is subject to the "withness of the body." Ecstasy seekers may underline the essence of the skier's joy in flight, but the honest man with the magnifying glass calls to mind the early clumsiness, the tight bootstrap, the burn of the cold in the nostril, the tremendous differential between image or ideal of the athlete and the actual gross accomplishment. This is what Schwartz does in the poem about his body, "The heavy bear who goes with me" (101). Only the speed of the imagination makes the body clumsy by comparison. When the poet wishes a gentleness or a refined nuance, a delicate touch, he can rely on the "heavy bear" to coarsen the moment:

> Stretches to embrace the very dear
> With whom I would walk without him near,
> Touches her grossly . . .
> . . . .
> Dragging me with him in his mouthing care,
> Amid the hundred million of his kind,
> The scrimmage of appetite everywhere. (101–02)

This vision is possible only because of the mind/body separation allowed for the sake of the poem and because of the respect for the ability the poet has for self-consciousness to an extreme. Part of the poet is assessing another part. The dichotomy is not meant as a piece of metaphysics, only a sharp observation. What comes out of it is that the body fits us like an ill-used shoe—clumsy, betraying, belying, distorting. Its needs are crude but powerful. The implication is that it cannot be relied upon for solace. And so the poet weights the matter. There are no doubts that this poem constitutes a firm, authentic portrayal. It is possible, however, to point out that if the body is forever with us with its liabilities, it has as its assets that—more often than not with most human beings—constitute profound consolation no matter how simple and brainless they appear. In its mildest form, for instance, the stroking need when gratified can be a solace. Thus, if this were the point of the poem, one could take the weighting as a serious fault in the portrayal. But the real point is simply the fact of the body in the world. The body is there, and it is there first just as art is there before criticism. The persistence alone is unending discomfort but his is a persis-

tence below the level of sex or food satisfaction: "Perplexes and affront with his own darkness, / The secret life of belly and bone" (101).

It should also be noted that this includes the clown motif that recurs often in Schwartz's poetry, usually supplied by one who distrusts strongly who feels especially vulnerable. Schwartz involved himself in a complex circuit of reactions that were meant to gain control and approbation. If he exaggerated his defect, admitted his clown-self, the admission put him on a level transcending the fault and thus he was automatically exonerated. I is not an uncommon way of exploiting a liability. The plus response is the promise first, then the performance of candidness. It could be labeled the *Ecce Homo* motif and is used for all it is worth in this well-known poem and also quite frequently in the rest of his work. This is not to say that truth is bypassed. On the contrary, much is revealed that is often elsewhere suppressed, but it is a mode based on selectivity and magnification. Behind it is a mask of irony and behind that the author moves in impregnable and perfect control. Looked at this way, and if one wished to take an extreme position, he might call the point of view "somewhere a lie," the result of a confused notion of truth, in somewhat the same fashion that the English philosopher takes his stand with "ordinary language" as against the confusions of sophisticated semanticists and traditional idealists.

In the tenth poem of the series, the reader is back to the unique self that combines, in poem five, both generals and particulars. In poem five, one was already introduced to the dog that is Shakespearean and to the children who are strangers. The tenth poem begins, "A dog named Ego," which is also referred to, some lines further, as "the stranger, unknown" (103). Recourse for solace is not being made to the complete ego that, in some way beyond us all, combines the poles of classification, is both concrete and abstract, unique, specific, particular and yet general and unfree: " 'Not free, no liberty, rock that you carry,' / So spoke Ego in his cracked and harsh voice" (103). Ego's voice is cracked and harsh not only because he is a dog—and there are connotations here—but also because in the clinical sense he lacks the other portion of the psyche, the Id, that was covered in poem nine and certain kinds of feeling that were reviewed in poem five. Ego, the dominator, buttressed with consciousness and reason, says,

> "Mine is the kingdom,
> Dynasty's bone: you will not be free,
> Go, choose, run, you will not be alone." (103)

Commensurate with his doghood is the "bone," but, preceded by the "dynasty's," this has all the implications of Schwartz's concern with origins and ancestry as powerfully determining factors in the destruction of freedom of will. Also, the dog is surrounded by snowflakes:

> "Come, come, come," sang the whirling snowflakes,
> Evading the dog who barked at their smallness,
> . . . .
> Falling from some place half believed and unknown. (103)

From heaven? From an origin beyond the capacity of ego alone to discover, known only by faith, which is beyond ego? Led by the dog, Ego, who chases the snowflakes, the poet goes

> further and farther away,
> While night collapsed amid the falling,
> And left me no recourse, far from my home,
> And left me no recourse, far from my home. (103)

Far from the possibility of solace through Ego, the poet instead experiences a very dangerous circumstance; he is lost, far from his home. What causes this in the terms of the poem is given in this line: "While Ego barked at them, swallowed their touch." This is a dire prediction for Schwartz, as hindsight now proves. Ego seeks to enlarge by incorporation. He would devour all the beautiful but cold experiences that fall unpredictably along his way. This is the way of Ego and if he is allowed to lead, the total human being can become lost with "no recourse" far from his home. Obviously there is no solace in the forward drive of Ego. His method is incorporation and what he tries to incorporate is evanescent; it liquefies and disappears, leaving him at a loss. So far as the literary artist is concerned, this mode of ego-leadership will not do either. Only the Eliotic solution of humility before tradition can save, and perhaps Schwartz was too honest in the context of his origin or too stiff-backed to accept it.

The final poem is headed "Dedication in Time," a proper heading, and since the first stanza concerns itself with mortality, a proper pun. Here, at the close of the eleven poems, the fugal subject is again stated but not implicitly. The added and substantiating element, such as has constituted the marrow of each restatement of the subject, begins in the second stanza, "Abide with me: do not go away" (104). All efforts at gaining solace have failed; there is none. But since there is none, perhaps, at the very least, he can have company in his misery: "Stay, then, stay! Wait now for me, / Deliberately, with care and circumspection" (104). And the only way he can have company is when the company is faithful within the dynamic process, that is, faithful to each movement within the dynamic process, that is, faithful to each movement in "the dance":

> When we are in step, running together,
> Our pace equal, our motion one,
> Then we will be well. . . . (104)

Parallel descent may yield "togetherness." There are times when a fugue will seem to end and then slow down a bit and drag out at the end. Here the theme of flux so wonderfully presented in poem four would seem to make a hysterical and appropriate ending: "We cannot stand still: time is dying, / We are dying: Time is farewell!" (104). But the poem slows all the way down to the one-word line "Stop," then slowly picks up and, for the first time in the section, ends on a forlorn although mildly positive note. In the fugue this is called "Picardy three." What may have held minor notes is ended on a major note, adding a firmness and uplift to the feeling of completion. And so this poem, and the fugal imitation, closes:

> Walking together on the receding road,
> Like Chaplin and his orphan sister,
> Moving together through time to all good. (104)

Closet Dramas

"Dr. Bergen's Belief"

Delmore Schwartz wrote only three closet dramas, although he was intensely interested in the field. The idea of looking and being looked at, which involved his extreme self-consciousness, while not an obsession, was frequently expressed in his work either explicitly in the comment or implicitly in his choice of form. His famous first story "In Dreams Begin Responsibilities" makes use of a dramatic device: the author writes about himself in a theater at the age of nine watching a movie showing the early days of his parents' courtship. Schwartz's long poem "Coriolanus and His Mother" again shows the poet watching and commenting on a presentation of Shakespeare's *Coriolanus*.

The three Schwartz plays are concerned with the problems of value and belief in our time. The first, "Dr. Bergen's Belief," partly prose and partly poetry, sets up a situation that must, dialectically, end in death; the second, *Shenandoah*, ends in life, the newborn babe; and the third, "Paris and Helen," closes on possibility or hope. All three are "existential" in the fundamental sense that they recognized the irreducibility of the individual and the absurdity of his circumstance. Of the three, the most significant is "Paris and Helen" which introduces not the anti-hero but the non-hero. Because these plays contain fine poetry and because they deal with problems that are part of the contemporary theater, they deserve notice. Many of our young poets write closet dramas, few are published, and fewer given any attention.

The plot of "Dr. Bergen's Belief" is straightforward and uncomplicated. Dr. and Mrs. Bergen have had two daughters; the older one has recently committed suicide. Dr. Bergen believes that she killed herself because of one of the doctrines of a new religion which he had set up a year before and of which she was an adherent. He believes that she could not fully enough examine her heart to know what she really wanted of life and that, in obedience to his doctrines, she sought an intuitive understanding using the perspective of death. Mrs. Bergen is ready to have him committed unless he drops the support of both the religion *and* the disciples, many of whom he is supporting. She complains bitterly about him to Dr. Newman, her daughter's doctor. There is a ritual service of the new religion held by Dr Bergen and his nine disciples, which is witnessed by Mrs. Bergen, Dr Newman, and Anthony, his oldest daughter's fiancé. After the service, Dr Bergen and Dr. Newman argue about the plausibility of Dr. Bergen's belief, the intuitions and convictions, and whether or not they are capable of proof. His daughter's death is brought up by Dr. Bergen in behalf of his point of view, and this backfires devastatingly when Dr. Newman shows a letter he received from the daughter in which she confesses that she killed herself because of her hopeless love for a married man. Shocked and beaten by Dr. Newman's revelation, Dr. Bergen, still announcing faith in his beliefs, and seeking to gain a further perspective, leaps over the balustrade to his death fifteen stories below.

The work starts with an introduction, a speech by Dr. Bergen that sets forth the theme of the play. The key word in the title of the play is "belief." "Bergen," which in German means "mountains," implies "heights" which, in turn, are rarefied, and this implies ideals and abstractions, usually part of any act of belief. A more direct connection between the name and the theme comes to light a bit later in the play: the central religious insight of Dr. Bergen is that the sky is the great blue eye of God.

He begins with a simple statement of disappointed belief, "there is no Santa Claus" (141). Equated with this statement is the following, "A final emptiness confronts your eyes" (141). This was written a long time after Matthew Arnold, more than a decade after "The Waste Land," and before the publication of Allen Tate's "Sonnets at Christmas." The alternative then and now, but perhaps not in the future, is that without belief there is only emptiness. Thus Schwartz moves to broaden the theme. The posture of prayer is like that of "The sad comedian of cane and derby" (142). "Prayer," he writes, "is now / Ridiculous" (142). No image of forgiveness, justice, loving kindness, and good will is possible any longer. Instead, the reader is returned from the "Bergen" of image and ideal to the concrete particular: "One knows that heaven is epiphenomenal / Rising from peaked musicians with bad complexions" (142).

Dr. Bergen affirms the need for belief and he promises to speak out. He knows us all, knows what we want, "Which is, though vaguely, all" (143), and he lists the countless needs and desires, but "None of these things are given. . . . [Y]ou get / What you do not want, what you do not need" (143). We get patience and naiveté, and hope, "Perplexed affection, inexhaustible will" (143). Then he asks the ultimate question, "What is this life? What can man ask to have?" (143).

He has asked his question, and now in the same comparatively artless fashion he must deliver his answer. So—the play begins. In extremely irregular pentameter, Anthony makes the opening speech; he complains that he cannot understand the unhappiness that must have driven Eleanor to her death. He criticizes her father and his disciples:

> —Here they construct a system to make their lives
> Self-regarding, self-gratifying, self-conscious,
> Indulging their minds in the old foolishness,
> The vain vanity: to correct the heart of man. . . . (144)

This, in his initial years of writing, could well be a statement of Schwartz's own aim. What comes out of a full consideration of his work is that he is a teacher and poet who, driven by impulses toward purism and extremes, limited, nevertheless, by self-consciousness and what he refers to as "selfhood," tends toward didacticism and seership. Schwartz *was* shamelessly "self-regarding"—his form of honesty—certainly "self-gratifying," and always "self-conscious." All of this revolves around "self." When the activity of the "self" is dictated by such concerns and when this is seen from the outside, it is invariably called "indulging." As for the word "foolishness," Schwartz was never one to hide his own and frequently exhibited it in the form of caricature or clowning, in several places explicitly referring to himself as a clown.

This should not act to diminish Schwartz as a man or a writer. His monumental honesty, his insistence on personal integrity, and his vitality and charm have been noted elsewhere and are here noted again. His importance as a writer is a stipulation of this work. These matters are mentioned only to help one surprise the young Schwartz at his work, to delve as accurately as possible into aim and motivation. "Dr. Bergen's Belief" is the oddest piece of writing published by a good poet of Schwartz's generation. I suggest that it is very close to the poet himself, that it is, in essence, a ritual monologue, weakly dramatized by characters who are not characters, and an allegory acting out intellectual and emotional problems that revolve around Schwartz's inability to believe. It contains contradictions, partly because rich symbolization is always ambiguous, but also because the author himself was troubled by contradiction. Schwartz was an intellectual square like Thomas Mann and was fascinated as the clear and sound body

of his thought and feeling gradually moved into areas of greater ambiguit
and more formidable contradiction. There are minds, like André Gide's, fc
instance, that entertain such anomalies with greater ease. There are othe
minds, like Rimbaud's, that bring no solid body of assimilated dogma t
oppose contradiction and that, therefore, accept it, simply, as reality.

In "Dr. Bergen's Belief" Schwartz deliberately presents a manifestl
impossible belief, but one that nevertheless bears a powerful moral aspec
If the sky is the eye of God, then we are all under constant surveillance. W
do nothing that is not looked at. The poet makes use of this in a later poen
"Starlight like Intuition Pierced the Twelve," that is about the effect create
on His disciples by the life of Christ, the refrain of which is " 'No matte
what we do, he looks at it!' " (*Vaudeville for a Princess* 47). If we are see
at all times—except at night when the eye is closed—then each action ha
weight and must stand judgment.

It follows, naturally, that the religious service starts with "imperative[s]
(151) and Dr. Bergen reads the disciples "this week's version of our fir
imperative" (151). If one understands that the prose paragraphs of the im
peratives are really vows and comments made to himself by the poet–
values, aims that a young writer might write in his notebooks—rather tha
a code suggested for all humankind as the imperative purports to be, the
these ideas lose their quality of oddness, becoming less pretentious an
more open to acceptance and criticism.

The disciples are told to be carefully conscious of what happens to the
from moment to moment, of all they do, of all that is done to them, to t
self-conscious "of the complexities of the personal event" (151), writin
all that happens at night in a book, reading the book later with "sham
remorse, and astonishment." A true and wonderful dictum follows:

> Do not be concerned with the false tone, the affected phrasing,
> the necessary pretentiousness of all self-consciousness.

> But deny the desire to invent, distort, defend, omit, forget, when
> confronted with your own foolishness. (151)

There is no doubt that in Schwartz's case he followed this prescription.
could not, however, be relied upon to be a perpetual shield, an apology
explanation for other omissions and transgressions. It is strong as a dictu
but thin, weak, and ultimately destructive as a mode for any and all occ
sions. It is all very well to give one's kingdom for a horse, but a sing
horse can only carry one so far.

The second imperative continues the effort of self-awareness and adds articulation" (154) to it. Again the disciples are cautioned to sharpen their awareness of what happens to them. They are told again to speak out without hesitation, without fear of arousing resentment or being laughed at, for frankness, sincerity, articulation, explicitness are the attributes of the man aware that God's blue eye regards him" (154). Taken at the fundamentalist level, this seems like an admission that judgment from above is necessary if human beings are to act as their best selves. Taken metaphorically, can only mean that good and honest men are good and honest. Also, it is questionable whether the fear of God need necessarily involve articulateness. Silence is not a sign of slackness or evil.

"Adopt with voluntary act the naive, the ingenuous, the stupid" (154). This is a direct command to put on a mask, unless it means that one should accept those who are naive, etc. In the former case, it is in opposition to all the foregoing tenets that stress honesty and openness. In the latter, it is found in Thomas Aquinas, who proposed that spiritual perfection need not be involved with intellectual perfection. This is also to be found in the writings of other Christian mystics where it emphasizes love for all humankind, even for the lowest, and it is developed in Dostoevsky. It is Christian virtue that is being emphasized—really in contradistinction to most of Schwartz's tendencies which are of Judaic origin. In fact, in a line a bit further on at the close of this imperative, Schwartz writes, "Gross, clumsy, foolish. / Pride, dignity, assurance / Are nothing without the power of righteousness, but once righteous, / They are garments, sweet fruits, the best pleasures of man" (154). Here is phrasing reminiscent of the first testament. Also, they remind one of the aristocratic personal code by which Lafcadio rewarded and punished himself in *Lafcadio's Adventures*, originally called *The Vatican Hoax* by André Gide.

The group now begins a part of the ritual that Dr. Bergen calls " 'Witness and Testimony' " (156). It refers to the innermost thoughts, cares, and observations of the disciples. These are spoken out at the meeting and commented on in a sentence or two by Dr. Bergen. Each gives testimony to the fact that he met some inner problem and by honesty and effort gleaned a lesson from it or, if it was odious, conquered it. One is reminded of a word, and the experience for it, that is current today: *confrontation*.

The testimonials continue. At the close, Martha, Eleanor's sister, remarks that in a dream she was trying to open Eleanor's forehead and look inside and that "I told her how noble she had been to kill herself and how it had helped all of us" (160). Here is the third sign of disintegrating effect that Dr. Bergen's belief has on the members of his family—the first bein his wife's distress for him; the second, his older daughter's demise. Th remark is altogether out of place, showing little appropriate feeling. Th belief is emphasized not the person, which is also contrary to the precep of the religion itself. Martha believes with Dr. Bergen that "She kille herself because she had come to the impasse where she could not unde stand her own heart . . . except by examining her heart in the perspective death" (160). It should be made clear, at this point, that Schwartz tru believed—and not without much to be said for it—that one should imag natively realize the fact of one's death as continuously as possible and se everything against this fact as backdrop. Such a notion comes to mar American readers with a shock; after all, we are part of a society that a cents youth. Death for Americans is smothered under a pile of euphemism Witness the elaborate efforts to make the acceptance of the "transition" a smooth and unnoticeable as possible. Except for the one appropriate mo ment in the velvet chapel, rawness and feeling are discouraged.

Naturally, then, the less said honestly about the transition to nothing ness, the better. Thus, one would expect that the center of Dr. Bergen belief, honesty prevailing, would certainly encompass a realistic attitud toward death. But this is not so, and Martha and Dr. Bergen insist on color ing Eleanor's death, on exploiting it for the sake of doctrine, and, mor profoundly, for their own sakes, for the perpetuation of the metaphysic (which, it turns out, protects them from the necessity of suffering the trutl at least for a time). This falsity at the core of all the protestations of hor esty must exist because the honesty is set, also, in a context that is th society in which they are living. Just as amelioration, compromise, an cover up exist in the society, the attempt to fight against it suffers from th very same disease. As Schwartz points out by the action of the play, th flight to metaphysics, dogma, and ideal, although seemingly noble, since is incomplete, is about as effective as the action of ostriches. And just a devastating.

The idea that a sense of history lends a fuller actuality to our appreher sion of life and prevents the present from distorting the view occurs ofte in Schwartz's poetry, but it is nowhere more beautifully expressed than i Eleanor's song, which is played for the disciples on the Victrola:

> I said, as by the river, we
> Gazed at the sliding water's gray,
> "This life's a dream, as others say,

A dream confirmed when memory
Holds up the past and dims the day,
As in the future we shall see
The present quickly passed away,
Irrelevant to our belief,
Misunderstood as every play,
Full of a secret actuality
Which worked its wish consummately
And held the conscious will at bay." (161)

The play is about to close; Dr Bergen engages Dr. Newman in an argument about his belief, admitting, finally, that it is based on intuition, can be neither proven nor disproven. He speaks with certainty, with exaltation, and one is inexorably reminded of Woodrow Wilson at the height of his idealistic misconceptions. Smiling with assurance, Dr. Bergen says, "I have direct experiences of what I assert, the only means of arriving at certainty" (165). Dr. Newman withholds no longer; he tells him, in brief, that Eleanor committed suicide for no reason other than that she was hopelessly in love with a married man who had no intention of leaving his wife. To prove his contention Dr. Newman shows Dr. Bergen a letter from Eleanor that was posted only an hour before her death. In it she admits her reason for killing herself and adds that she is allowing her father to believe what he wishes about the matter because in that way she will at least be useful for once. Dr. Bergen appears humbled for a moment. Anthony, the betrayed fiancé, delivers a speech in which he comments on himself and illusion. In it he brings up the matter of belief:

Belief contrives
A curious house, peculiar pyramid
Which narrows as it must to nothingness.
And on that tiny top we stand until
The actual sand shifts as it must, betrays
The desert of our lives, our broken sleep. (167–68)

The subject is betrayal by belief. But Dr. Bergen does not accept this: "That does not apply to me. I did not deceive, I was not deceived, except by one poor miserable distraught girl. . . . But I was not deceived in all, only in her" (168). He steps from the long table to the parapet and tells the group that he, too, will kill himself because he is sincere, because "The horror of doubt crowds my mind and I cannot endure it" (169). He explains that he went, in his life, from one type of partial satisfaction to another until, one day, he suddenly realized the pure fact that the moment was continuously and relentlessly approaching when he would die, when his body would rot. He spent a year in the deepest despondency until he began to undergo the special experiences that gave him his insight and belief and changed all. Now he has nothing left but the will to know. As several scream, he jumps to his death. Rakovsky, one of his disciples, Anthony, and Dr. Newman each in order make one remark at the close of the curtain.

Rakovsky . . . :
Knowledge and belief devour the mind of man.

Anthony:
Belief, knowledge, and desire—desire most of all.

Dr. Newman:
Man destroys his own heart. (171)

So ends this play—on the problem of belief. It is peculiarly cramped as a play, partly because there is not much conflict or plot, but mainly because there is no characterization. The dialogue, as stated earlier, is really a monologue in prose and poetry. The conflict between abstract or metaphysical ideal and concrete reality, between the need to believe even in the most outlandish notions and the necessity to do without, has been stated many times in works of art. Don Quixote comes to mind as a fuller, richer figure, clothed in nobility and romance not vouchsafed to Dr. Bergen. Compared to Quixote, Bergen's is a narrow, self-centered viewpoint and this is, perhaps, as it should be, for the author—if the double-suicide plot means anything—means to show the danger in certain kinds of needs to believe.

Shenandoah

After "Dr. Bergen's Belief," Schwartz published two more verse plays, *Shenandoah* and "Paris and Helen." Both of these appeared two years after the first in 1941. This interim seems to have allowed for a ripening. In *Shenandoah* Schwartz addresses himself to a theme that is part of his own Jewish heritage; it is a moving play. The verse is fuller, more substantial than in his first play. Put another way, the poet is not afraid of admitting the fullness of the iambic pentameter and of making use of it. His earlier blank

verse is evasive, as if he wished to create a spanking new sound, a sophis-
tication that frequently leaves his lines flat or prosy. In *Shenandoah* his
orotund ideas find ample voice.

Shenandoah presents the ritual performed at the time that the child is
circumcised and named. It is a ceremony of great dignity. All rituals of
naming are concerned with esoteric meaning, the feeling of deep-lying
significance, therefore, with meaning and, most important, ultimate mean-
ing. If "Dr Bergen's Belief," Schwartz's first play, lays bare the failure of
ultimate belief in our time even when the ability to believe is not lost, then,
in *Shenandoah* Schwartz offers a play that also celebrates the significance
that is involved with an ultimate belief—naming a newborn son.

The importance of the naming, both everyday and magical, is made
clear by the family discussions and the presence throughout the play of the
mature Shenandoah as commentator on the proceedings. Certainly Schwartz
takes none of the suggestions of T. S. Eliot in his essay "Tradition and the
Individual Talent"; there is never an abeyance of the personal or a channel-
ing of the personal through the traditional. If some recent trends in con-
temporary poetry are identified as "confessional poetry," then Schwartz
should be recognized as the modern father of the school. But in *Shenandoah*
alone, he allows himself the palliative of fairly traditional blank verse and
an occasional biblical phrasing and rhythm. *Shenandoah* is really one of
the best balanced works of this poet, in good part because of the leavening
nature of these two traditions that do mange to filter into it. He invites the
reader at the very beginning of the play:

> —Return to me, stand at my point of view,
> Regard with my emotion the small event
> Which gave my mind and gave my character,
> Amid the hundred thousand possibilities
> Heredity and community avail,
> Bound and engender,
> > the very life I know! (7)

Again, as in the short story "In Dreams Begin Responsibilities," he goes
back to his origins, as if origins explain everything: "The curtain rises on a
dining room / In the lower middle class in 1914" (7). Standing at an angle
to the scene, Shenandoah reviews his parents' marriage; the following qua-
train sums up much:

> How can two egos live near by all their days,
> If Love and Love's unnatural forgiveness
> Do not give to the body's selfishness
> And the will's cruelty lifelong *carte blanche*? (9)

He is passing judgment on his parents; the verse alternates between wryness and despair. Elsie, the mother, tells her father-in-law, Jacob Fish, that she would like to see the boy named Jacob in his honor: "She thinks to please her husband through his father. / Do not suppose this flattery too gross" (11). But Jacob demurs, reminding her that in this new America she has forgotten the customs of her people. To name the child after a relative who is alive is unlucky; it could be Jacob Fish's death warrant. Elsie says that she is surprised that he believes such superstitions. Shenandoah comments, "How powerful the past! O king of kings" (10). For Schwartz, the past is all-powerful and determining.

There is some altercation and Elsie decides to change the name of the child, even though the name has already been engraved on expensive announcements. She decides that "Jacob" is not a fine name anyhow, and she wants an unusual name, "because he is going to be an unusual boy" (11). Elsie hands the child, who will be named "Shenandoah," to Shenandoah the adult to hold, symbolically giving him for the brief instant, before the past takes its firmest hold on him, his freedom; he holds his own life in his hands. The spotlight falls on him and he addresses the child,

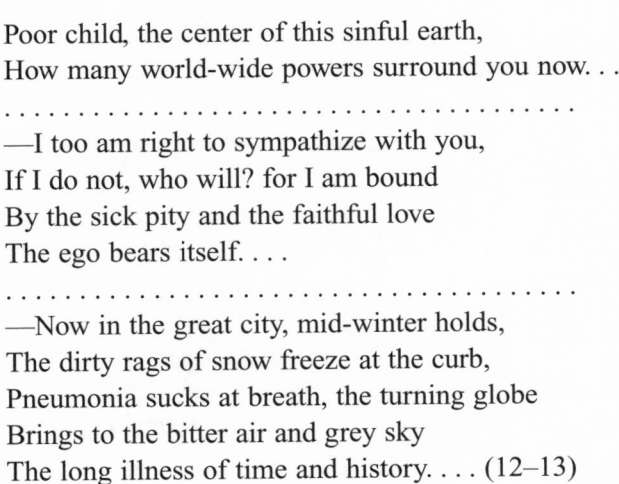

> Poor child, the center of this sinful earth,
> How many world-wide powers surround you now. . . .
> . . . .
> —I too am right to sympathize with you,
> If I do not, who will? for I am bound
> By the sick pity and the faithful love
> The ego bears itself. . . .
> . . . .
> —Now in the great city, mid-winter holds,
> The dirty rags of snow freeze at the curb,
> Pneumonia sucks at breath, the turning globe
> Brings to the bitter air and grey sky
> The long illness of time and history. . . . (12–13)

In many ways, Schwartz's self-consciousness becomes over-defensive and he himself anticipates what might be said about a statement he makes, this giving him the material for his next statement. The effect is of a too-bright self-consciousness that can be, in the long run, alienating to the reader. When a person gets too defensive and speaks self-deprecatingly, the auditor is handed a burden of expostulation—to deny the charge; this gets in the way of any possible sympathy. Too much of it, although it stems from the need to be omniscient, ends up with the reader irritatedly feeling that he is dealing with mere cleverness. More important, however, is the fact that it stops feeling. If Schwartz has ended the statement in the center of the fourth line quoted and merely said, "If I do not [sympathize with you], who will?" the overtones from Hillel, "If I am not for myself, who is for me?" would have helped the reader toward the profound and biblical emotion that should surround the ritual. The interruption, "for I am bound / By the sick pity," preserves Shenandoah's omniscience, a joy for Schwartz at the expense of true reader participation.

The speech actually ends with an apology, to my mind in very bad taste, taken from the epigraph to "Gerontion" by T. S. Eliot:

> —Forgive my speech: I have nor youth nor age,
> But as it were an after-dinner speech,
> Speaking of both, with endless platitudes— (13)

The double apology, Eliot's and then his own addition, "with endless platitudes," seems nothing if not foolish. It is, in a way, kicking the pail over, and a speech full of nobility and beauty ends up being mouthed by a clown.

A general discussion of desirable names ensues. They decide to go through the social columns of the newspaper to see what powerful American names are mentioned. Shenandoah observes wryly:

> While they gaze at their glamorous ruling class,
> I must stand here, regardant at an angle,
> I must lie there, quite helpless in my cradle,
> As passive as a man who takes a haircut—
> And yet how many minds believe a man
> Creates his life *ex nihilo,* and laugh
> At the far influence of deities,
>   and stars— (14)

"Regardant" is right, for it means "face in profile and looking backwards." This makes the identification complete for, of course, it is only the grown shadow-self of Shenandoah that can look backward, not the infant, or if it is the infant—and one can maintain the thought momentarily—it strikes one with dismay and even terror, almost a perspective, as Kenneth Burke might say, by incongruity.

During the course of the discussion a Mr. Brewster is mentioned who "has an estate in the Shenandoah Valley" (15). Elsie Fish cries, "Shenandoah! What a wonderful name: Shenandoah Fish!" (15). Then, a marvelous stage direction: "[*The baby begins to howl.*]" And quickly Shenandoah says,

> Now it is done! Quickly! I am undone:
> This is the crucial crime, the accident
> Which is more than an accident. . . . (15)

Here follows a disquisition in pentameter on the folklore of naming, how primitive peoples are apt to call a child by a demeaning adjective such as "Filth" or "Nothingness" (Jews avoid saying a child is beautiful) "In order to outwit the evil powers" (16); how a child is often named after his father, "the wish is clear, / All men would live forever" (16); how some are named after places, "tacit / Admission of the part the *milieu* plays" (16); how Jews were wise to call God " 'The Nameless' " (16); how it is right that legal codes make name-change (identity-change) difficult. There is more, but this is sufficient to show the rich textures of the discussion that ends with Shenandoah's notion of how one should be named, the touching and plaintive, "let each child choose his name / When he is old enough" (16). He proposes it with charming diffidence, for a change, making it a question, inviting the reader's agreement rather than insisting on it.

They discuss, they quarrel, his Uncle Nathan tries to tell his father how unsuitable the name is for the child ("Don't you see how pretentious the name is?" [19]), and Shenandoah, watching the argument, philosophizes on the fact that men who should be creating works of art, making friends or love, instead prefer conflict ("hate / May seem the energy which drives the stars" [20]). He is fascinated by the multiplicity of causes that are at work in the room to fashion the future of this child.

> —It is impossible to tell you now
> How many world-wide causes work this room
> To bring about the person of your name. . . . (20)

This provided an opportunity to make a figure that might help with the analysis of Schwartz's habit of mind, which could be called "square" or "dated" or "at a distant focus." Here he is overwhelmed by the multiplicity of causes. This is certainly overwhelming as long as one makes the unit of measurement "causes." It is then as hard as spooning out the ocean. Similarly, Schwartz, in his work, seems to require a traditional order to thinking and its presentation. As he grew older, he tried to encompass many kinds of disorder with his fundament of discursive Western logic and became overwhelmed with the complication of countless contradictions at the heart of everything. If, in the first example above, he were to abandon the use of the idea of "causes" altogether, he would not need to be overwhelmed.

This is not meant to be a philosophical argument; this is merely another attempt to communicate the nature of Schwartz's approach to writing and thinking. Henri Bergson said that if we classify the motion of an arm rising, we get a description of millions of changes—air motions, blood movements, force exerted, epidermal reactions, muscular shifts. But if our description says simply "The hand is lifted," we avoid, assuming we wish to, the overwhelming details that classifying brings with it. This holds as well for Schwartz when he struggles to fit occurrences today into the four-square net he fashioned from the writings of the great men of the past who, as Shenandoah says in this speech, "will obsess this child when he can read" (20). Schwartz has created a closed system; he has made *himself* a closed system. No matter how widely he appears to open himself to new ideas, how voraciously he seems to devour new cultural experiences, the matrix is already formed and really not open to change. There is in such a formation only the *appearance* of flexibility: no matter now rich the content, the form remains fixed. In spite of the tremendous intake, the balloon only gets larger, but it always remains round.

Shenandoah's speech continues telling the whereabouts of each of the great mean at the very time. He is naming the coordinates of the matrix. The interesting fact is not the list of men, but that they help to constitute a pressuring of perspective that he brings to bear at every point in his examination of life. One would suppose that nothing is wrong with this. It seems to be a solid identity-formation, culturally speaking, but it is the very solidity that makes the Achilles heel. The earnest pressing of this point on all occasions prevents the light touch, ever, and, more important, the special creativity of the poet never escapes this direct pressure. It is never allowed to frisk about, to bring the indirect into play, to bring fragmented and devious modes into operation. All becomes closed and heavy-handed with the results that Schwartz's writing often seems dated by comparison with work that allows tangents. Shenandoah names Joyce, Pound, Picasso, Rilke, Kafka, Perse, and Mann, "Declaring the agony of modern life," and he closes the speech:

> This child will learn of life from these great men,
> He will participate in their solitude,
> And maybe in the end, on such a night
> As this, return to the starting-point, his name,
> Showing himself as such among his friends— (21)

A great hope, and affecting, especially in view of Schwartz's career disappointment. And this very hope is stated solemnly, surely—preformed in a closed system—ironically part of the fault that prevented its realization.

Ironically, too, Shenandoah's father checks with his attorney, a man for whom the father is a paying client, one who is bullied into saying the name is a fine one. So the child will pay for another flaw in his father's character. Shenandoah underscores the circumcision rite as appropriate.

> for with a wound
> —What better sign exists—the child is made
> A Jew forever! . . .
> . . . .
> —Chosen for wandering and alienation
> In every kind of life, in every nation— (27)

The play ends with the poet's seeking refuge only in "Transient release . . . in the darkened theater's plays. . . ." (28).

"Paris and Helen"

The same year that *Shenandoah* appeared, 1941, the New Directions Press published, in its annual compendium of new writing, *New Directions in Prose and Poetry*, another verse play by Schwartz, "Paris and Helen." So far as published work is concerned, this play is the last of its genre Schwartz wrote. His eighteen closely penciled notebooks contain no other part of a play.

Although it is cut out of the same prosodic cloth as *Shenandoah*, "Paris and Helen" is more closely related to Schwartz's poem "Coriolanus and

His Mother." Its theme is a dialectical continuation from this poem: if Coriolanus is the hero, Paris is the non-hero. In the poem, the impasse of the uncompromising hero is resolved by death; in this verse play, the crisis of the *compromising* hero is ended by escape from death. Coriolanus rejects the flesh in favor of the image; Paris rejects the image of the hero in favor of the flesh. It is possible to see this as a further step in the narcissist's progress, the playwright's making a gesture of maturity, seeming to open somewhat, to surrender a little to the invasion of the unpredictable, uncontrollable aspect of reality.

Also Schwartz has an involvement with being looked at, the relationship between the actor and the audience. A natural result of this preoccupation, combined with his struggle to bridge the real and the ideal, is his identification of the clumsy, accidental, wanton aspects of reality with the crude figures of popular entertainment. Thus, "Paris and Helen" is subtitled "an entertainment," and it is inscribed "to Metro-Goldwyn-Mayer." This looks backward to "Chaplin and his orphan sister" ("The Repetitive Heart" 104) and forward to his flyleaf comment in *Vaudeville for a Princess*, "Suggested by Princess Elizabeth's admiration of Danny Kaye" (1).

Schwartz is perpetually attracted to the difference and distance between the real and the ideal, and he persists in presenting repeated resolutions of this problem. This enactment includes Schwartz himself on his persona (in "Paris and Helen," he is the Dramatist), the actors, and at least references to the audience if not, as in "Coriolanus and His Mother," the audience itself, and all of this is formed into the verse play as exorcism, talisman, strategy.

Nevertheless, the Coriolanus image stubbornly prevails. This is clear in the sarcasm and disdain with which the prospect of writing a "popular" piece is considered at the beginning of the play in the conversation of the Producer and the Dramatist:

> But how can I compete with the whores of the mind,
> So dominant upon the Great White Way,
> Sleeping with all the ticket agencies? (196)

Even though the dramatist says wryly, "O, I would write one, *if I could!*" (196), later in the play he cries longingly,

> all of us would be the noble Hector
> If we but could? Paris himself would rather
> Be like the noble Hector, *if he but could!*

The contempt in the capitalization of "The Great White Way" is obvious; and it is clear that instead of Coriolanus, in this play we have Hector who is of the same heroic cast.

The play presents the intervention of the Goddess, Venus, into the Helen-Paris-Menelaus triangle at the point where Paris must face Menelaus in combat before the walls of Troy. The relationship of these characters and the kind of sex that intrudes are suggested by Schwartz's casting of the characters: Paris to be played by Robert Montgomery; Helen by Madaleine Carroll; Hector by Spencer Tracy; and Venus alternately by Greta Garbo, Myrna Loy, Hedy Lamarr, and Dame Mae Whitty. The Producer challenges the Dramatist in the first scene to write a popular success, insisting that regardless of the Dramatist's high standards, he is "flesh and blood like the rest of us" (195). The Dramatist's mind goes back in history, searching the past for a story, and lights on Homeric Troy, "The very early morning of Western culture" (197). He will be able to use the Trojan story because it will arouse the interest of everyone, since "sexual congress is the story's nub" (197). At this point the Producer interrupts:

> Is all this platitude quite necessary?
> The audience is waiting for the play—
> (*Impatient claps from the audience*.) (198)

The conversation is transpiring before the curtain and the parentheses bring an audience into the theater, "alienating" the reader in the sense that Bertolt Brecht used the word. Another level of looking has been added and the interruption takes one back to this device as it is used in "Coriolanus and His Mother," where the great culture heroes of the past interrupt the play with comments and are, in turn, interrupted by the author who steps forward before the curtain. No doubt riches accrue, but attention should be given to the fact that this compulsive addiction of viewers who are viewed, and viewers who are viewing viewers viewing, etc., makes an important part of the theme the passivity of the *voyeur*.

The scene moves on to the old men on the walls of Troy. They gossip about the beauty of Helen and the confrontation of Hector and Paris after Paris' shameful exit, which ended his contest with Menelaus. Again the Dramatist interrupts, comments on *their* comments. Again the matter of looking is brought up:

> Spectators, tourists, paid admissions,
> These old men have no more to do, but look . . .

> And yet they register the action's fullness—
> Because they are somewhat apart from it—
> Because they're old, because the past knows more—
>   (200)

The old men decide that regardless of her beauty, it would be better if Helen went back to Greece so that war might be avoided. The Dramatist ends the scene quoting an "expatriate American" who "wrote so well / Putting old Greek into modern English" (204), and the final remark of the Dramatist is, "How the past / Once in a poem, has more lives than a cat!" (204). Both the old men and the Trojan scene emphasize the power of the past that reaches through to the present in which the Dramatist is preparing his play.

Scene 2 reveals the old men describing the fight between Menelaus and Paris. A cloud of dust descends over Paris at the critical moment. He is protected and removed, leaving a raging and frustrated Menelaus on the field. The curtain descends and the Dramatist explains that this occurrence is "no sudden accident, mere cloud of dust" but "It is divinity itself which interferes" (208). Venus has given Paris protection because he once chose her as more beautiful than Juno or Diana, which insures his survival. The Dramatist takes occasion to excuse his presence, since it

> embellishes the whole
> With the rich views of a self-conscious mind. . . .
> . . . .
> This is the greatest virtue of all art
> That it possesses Life and yet transcends it— (208–09)

This is the fundamental statement in the scene; it does not pertain to the action of the play. It is concerned neither with the conflict nor the characters but with the Dramatist, and it places him comfortably on top of it all, in control where safety lies and where, unlike life, everything is arrangeable and predictable. The paradox lies in that in the very act of presenting a seeming confession of submissiveness and acceptance of life—identification with the non-hero, Paris—Schwartz arrogates to himself powers that make this truly impossible and that would seem to save him from the necessity of this identification. One is reminded of the ending of an earlier poem of his, "For the One Who Would Take Man's Life in His Hands":

"—What do all examples show?
What can any actor know?
The contradiction in every act,
The infinite task of the human heart."
(*In Dreams Begin Responsibilities* 120)

The non-hero, like Paris, wins by losing; Schwartz, the Dramatist, loses by winning.

The third scene demonstrates Paris' victory and analyzes its nature. The victory is survival, the means is Venus through Helen, the mode an unheroic abandonment of the battlefield for the bedroom. At the beginning of the scene Paris is returned to Helen safe and shamed; Helen upbraids him; he tells her not to be a child, points out that the next time he might win although today belongs to Menelaus:

For I have some divinities on my side, and it is all a matter of luck, or divinity, or something which has very little to do with one's character or effort. You ought to know that, you who were given your beauty effortlessly, and spontaneously. (211)

She tells him he speaks like a coward. He answers that he speaks like a "sensible, intelligent man" (211), and right here is breached the value structure supporting the heroic. "A matter of luck, or divinity, or something" implies an absence of the ordered cosmic framework on which values such as the heroic depend. The "divinity" mentioned has nothing to do with the distant, thunderous Zeus, but with the casual, the feminine (Venus), the whimsical, and the purchasable. It is a tangential view, wry, accepting, but one that insists, nevertheless, on one condition: "opting out" of the established ideal in favor of the immediately real. A man set against an image can cut a sorry figure, but after all, it is the man who breathes and loves.

Looking is again involved, for now Paris is unveiled for Helen to see. Rid once and for all the armor of image and ideal, this free man, the nonhero, desires as he never desired before, and tells Helen so. The naked truth desires and is desirable; Helen is equally aroused. The Dramatist holds up the action and underscores the moment:

O what insight this moment holds, that now
Desire should be the greatest,

now in the aftermath
Of worst defeat, immense humiliation. . . . (212)

He marvels at the triumph of Paris, who is "the average sensual man / One so much so he is a wonder at it" (213). He points out that this is the way things are, shows the similarity to the tremendous success enjoyed in America by the ignorant man largely because "He did not know or think of better things" (213). And he ends this speech sardonically trapping the reader into an identification with Paris as he addresses the audience *in the play*:

> Such is the way of the world, my dears,
> Passive and gazing, in the audience— (213)

There is a cry behind the curtain which rises to show that Paris' brother, Hector, has entered the bedroom, bent on murder. Paris defends himself with argument, finally telling Hector that the warrior ideal is used by the people to maintain their own prosperity, to back up "usurpations of this city on the whole countryside" (215); he italicizes *"That is all it is."* Nothing avails, so that Paris, in desperation tries to show Hector the full-bodied and naked truth of his motivation for survival, the unveiled Helen in her beauty. Hector is shaken by this argument, but feels contempt for Paris. Nothing concrete can change his mind and, mechanically, he proceeds to the murder of his brother. From Hector's point of view, Paris is contemptible, a coward, a shirker of responsibility, almost a degenerate. Again the Goddess of Love intervenes; Venus warns Hector, "This man is mine, Hector. *He shall not die*" (216). This "average sensual man" is to be saved! He thanks Venus, turns immediately to Helèn and says, "Do not weep. This is Life. This is how Life is." He is not speaking of abstraction or of Goddesses, but simply of the contingent nature of life, that whatever characteristics he happens to have happened to save him. There is the implication that what saves Paris saves the average man, the viewer, the non-hero whenever he *is* saved.

At curtain the Dramatist, who has made a great show of revealing the play within the play and spectator-watching spectator, peeks behind the curtain to watch. Paris and Helen are making love and he describes it, commenting at the same time on the fact that they are being looked at and that he is looking.

Voyeur! Voyeur! Voyeur! all men are but
Voyeurs! you in the audience most of all.

The Dramatist, no more than Schwartz, cannot resist a pun, so he adds,

here have we seen tonight
A grievous fight in which divinity
Hits heroism, as you saw, *below the belt*. (214)

And, in the closing remarks, one cannot escape, either, the powerful irony of

Is it not right
And just that strong divinity
Should intervene so much in human life? (214)

Here chance is characterized as sacred, divinity as accident.

It is not to the point, here, to evaluate "Paris and Helen" as a working play, although it is difficult to imagine it playing well. It is too synoptic, too dense, even for a one-act closet drama. On the other hand, it is not successful as a poem since the texture is too variegated—prose, poetry, pun, and characterization all in a few short pages. As the presentation of an insight into human nature, it is certainly concise, but a quality of poetic line is the only excuse for density, and in "Paris and Helen" even what seems dense at first proves in many cases to be merely indirect, far-fetched, or elliptical on close inspection. There is, however, a success here on another level. This little play is a modern reply to Jean Giraudoux, who explores the same general area in *Tiger at the Gates*. Almost in a Shavian tradition, Schwartz proffers common sense and the desire to love as opponents of Giraudoux's dramatic symbol of the inevitability of war. Both plays are involved with a sense of the absurd, Giraudoux's with a cynical acceptance and Schwartz's with a more positive resolution.

GENESIS

Genesis, Schwartz's third book of poetry, is an autobiography through the poet's fourth grade in school. The title should have a certain poignancy for those familiar with his earlier work. In this book Schwartz tells of his origin in some detail, but it is also an account of the genesis of his psychological difficulties and there is little doubt that, considering the poet's interest in Freudian theory and psychiatric therapy and his penchant for puns, he meant the title to have at least these two meanings. The book also contains reiterations of his basic themes, all the attitudes and problems of the grown man. This material is usually couched in verse while the autobiography, more often than not, is rendered in prose.

Although Schwartz makes the statement in a note to the reader in the beginning of the book that "This is the first book of a work which is almost finished" (vii), nothing further of this nature was published. Several surmises are possible: that this book says all he had to say on the subject; that he had more to say, but said it in his short stories; or that he was disappointed in the critical reception of the book and so never continued with it. But part of Schwartz's later illness expressed itself in an extraordinary degree of reticence about the facts of his adult life. It is pardonable to suggest that he was incapable of presenting it as directly as he did his childhood and background. Even about *Genesis* he protests in his introduction that "it is an obvious stupidity and misuse to take any sentence as the truth about any particular human being" (ix).

The fact remains that the biographical detail in *Genesis* recounts the background and early experiences of Delmore Schwartz. Since this is the case, *Genesis* gains in significance when some knowledge of Schwartz's later life is available. And even more important than the work, marriage, and publication data is the picture of Schwartz as a personality. It is the formation of this personality that the storyline of *Genesis* describes while the ideas and attitudes fully matured are presented through the poetic commentary. The arrangement of this work has caused it to be referred to by one critic as a blasphemous satire on the Bible. The parallel with the Book of Genesis is certainly clear, together with the biblical rhythm of the prose

and of some of the verse. But one can just as well see a parallel between
this structure and the Torah, which is composed of two main sections, the
text and the commentary. In *Genesis* the text is a prose story and the verse
is the commentary. By such a comparison or association, the origin of the
inescapably satirical note, the mock-heroic, is clearly seen. Later, as a kind
of post-hypnotic jolt, comes the realization of the degree of bitterness in a
man who, with such richness and love, mocks the reader and mocks him-
self as well.

Genesis opens with a "chorus of the dead," not so named by the poet but
nevertheless composed of the ghosts of the same culture heroes who at-
tended the play in his early poem "Coriolanus and His Mother." They wait
upon and witness the sleep and awakening in the morning of Hershey Green.
The time is around 1930, the young man in his late twenties. Hershey, with
their encouragement, begins, as if on the psychoanalyst's couch, to tell
them his story. Knowing Schwartz's interest in the power of the past, one is
not surprised to find the story begins with Hershey's grandfather, whom he
had never seen, in Russia during the final days of the Czarist regime, and
with his father describing their efforts to get to America. Jack Green,
Hershey's father, was assisted by his older brother, who had arrived in
America first. (Ben Newman, the man who ultimately became Jack Green's
father-in-law had, it appeared, deserted his wife and his own brother-in-
law, whose money he had taken and had used to come to America. Finally,
he paid off his brother-in-law and sent for his wife and family.) Jack Green
is described as a passionate, stubborn, self-centered man, and so he was if
he is to be taken as the projection of Harry Schwartz, Delmore Schwartz's
father. And Eva Green, nee Newman, represents the tactless, unhappy
woman who married Harry Schwartz and bore him two sons, Delmore and
Kenneth.

At the point where Eva Green has been married a year and where Jack
Green has already discovered that as far as he is concerned the marriage is
a mistake, the reader has reached page 46. The text has not been all plot;
the plot is confined to the prose section of single-sentence paragraphs. It
moves forward smoothly with a rhythm and vitality very much like the
stories of Sholem Aleichem. A semi-poetic and synoptic effect is achieved
partly by the fact that the paragraphs are ended even when the sentence is
not; it simply continues in the next paragraph, which is naturally indented
and starts with a capital. One would expect this to give it a quality similar
to prose poetry, but this is not the case. Here is an example of the unfin-
ished sentences at the end of a line:

And the idea grew in Noah's being, the idea sprang to the
conscious mind, many a care and means

Seemed to suggest itself. The soldiers by a fast-flowing river
one morning camped and went bathing.

Noah undressed with the rest and disposed his uniform where
it would be discovered. . . . (9)

These prose passages are interspersed with sections of the blank verse
commentary. The effort of the verse is to establish the self-consciousness
of the poet in America. But it is not only the concrete America of buildings
and space but a point in time, culturally speaking. Schwartz seems, through
his personae, to be attempting to fix the precise outlines of his individual-
ity. He is asking, in effect, what is the individual, what am I? The reply is in
the poetry. The individual is in the world and the world "is everything that
is the case." One, according to Schwartz (implicitly) and to Heidegger be-
fore him, does not exist without the other. Therefore, the province of po-
etry consists of every relationship—social, philosophical, religious, and
physical—of which the poet at the given point in time is capable. And the
given point is, for the poet, now and America.

The American Dream is for Americans, at the very least for second-
generation Americans. For the emigrant, for Ben Newman and Jack Green,
there is the promise that is the precursor of the Dream.

"Would you like to start from the womb again?
Here you can leave the womb a second time!
O here the world and Life begin afresh—" (19)

And

"The old dream of America springs up,
Springs like a boxer's arm, blocking a blow. . . ." (27)

The personalities of Jack Green and his brother, Albert, are described in
the verse,

"—Albert the family man, Jack passionate,
Passionate for himself and appetites—" (36)

Albert awakens one night and sees his brother's large strong frame stretched in sleep; immediately he resolves to urge Jack to be a policeman:

> "He knows by now how the world moves, he knows
> Many maneuvers of *Realpolitik*,
> He wakes his brother up to be a cop!" (36)

It does not take long for the young men to become Americans. But Jack begins to sell insurance, makes many friends whom he loses as soon as they discover that they were only charmed to the point of purchase; they were used. Jack's nature is revealed, thus, not only by the explicit comment and analysis but by episodes and images. Jack is restless, wishes to "settle down," begins to court Eva. He is welcomed by Eva but not by old Ben Newman, who senses the restlessness in his future son-in-law. The action is surrounded in the verse by "signs of the times,"

> "as if the pair
> Walked hand-in-hand upon a roof-top brink
> Fifty-five floors above the city street,
> As in the comedies of Harold Lloyd—" (47)

Not only movie stars, but cartoon characters—Mutt and Jeff, the Katzenjammer Kids—and popular legends like Santa Claus, all the paraphernalia of the popular American scene are mentioned, made use of by the poet in building the background from the stage on which his little ego will soon strut. Jack Green goes into the real estate business, making money from the hope of other recent arrivals from Europe. "He was surely a man who was going to be rich!" (53). Schwartz's recurrent theme involving his complex concern with choice is interpolated here for the first time in *Genesis*. It is in reference to the business moves made by Jack Green, who has been shown to be the kind of man who will "take his life in his hands" (*In Dreams Begin Responsibilities* 119).

> "I see now how Jack Green's life by his will
> Was made, yet, of necessity,
> By the great causes made essentially:
> Europe, America, Capitalismus. . . ."
> . . . .
> " '—Walking involves ground as well as legs!' " (53)

Here is interposed one of Schwartz's long philosophical passages that do impede the action but which are integral to the poetry. In this passage he is clear and explicit on the subjects of belief, determinism, significance, the hereafter. The hope and enthusiasm of youth still light up his doubts. It is back to the heights of this ebullience that his later, forced affirmations seek to take him. At this point nothing is forced; the excitement explodes of its own volition, as it were. For all the emotion, it is still a statement of complex and balanced doubts.

At the close of it, he falls back, nevertheless, on the only reliable salvation; at least he can have the joy of knowing. When, at a later date, *this* is finally destroyed, he encounters a despair that is only masked momentarily by his affirmations.

> "Perhaps the sum alone decides the life,
> And all the souls that are perhaps are spun
> Just like the roulette wheel or turning globe
> Under Time's utter fire and dazzling oars,
> —Perhaps the all decides and nothing less,
> The all immensely coiled and soiled. Perhaps
> The pure event leaps from the infinite cave. . . .
> . . . .
> —And if I say this from death's worst despair,
> I know that maybe God has purposes
> Stranger than any dream and wholly just,
> But now in ignorant death this is a thought
> My mind can utter but cannot believe,
> —Perhaps Eternity will light up all,
> Even the ignorance in which I grieve
> —It is impossible to know at all
> Until one knows causes and principles:
> . . . .
> O friends! this is the only happiness!
> Lo, in this Switzerland God has made clear
> Peaks, heights, and snows! how wonderful
> Is Life, O wonderful beyond belief,
> Hope, and desire, on Reason's far-off heights!
> —Ice cream and other sweets have gone away,
> All dreams are rags, all hopes have died. Only
> To see the causes which debauched our lives

In this eternity's cold cloudy light
Remains to us: let's make the most of it! . . ." (54–55)

The cold conclusions set off the center of vitality, happiness, enthusi-
asms, and warmth as night-black borders might set off a party invitation.
Schwartz is young but his mind is older. The emotion seems possible be-
cause there is hope, and hope is possible because of his youth. This sounds
something like the strong affirmations of his later poetry, but the balance
among hope, emotion, and reason is different and this difference is what
creates the quality of desperation in the later work. The final despair that
results in the feeling of forced yea-saying, and is in one sense, therefore,
meretricious, does not come into existence until later. What this amounts
to is that the later affirmations with their hysterical exultance have a differ-
ent purpose from that of early statements. They are masks and buttresses,
collapsing as they are erected. The emotion in this last quotation is of an-
other simpler order. Although it is already inappropriate to the message of
the mind around which it curls, inappropriate in the sense of the stock
responses that such insights usually call forth, it is appropriate in that, at
least, it is the exuberance of early vitality. The attitude in these lines is only
one key lower than Thomas Hardy's when he ends his poem, "I should go
with him in the gloom, / Hoping it might be so" (127).

The marriage between Jack and Eva Green limps along with Eva's grow-
ing less secure each day; she "had been told that a child kept a man at
home" (65). Her doctor explains that she will need surgery to make her
amenable to impregnation. She does not dare ask her husband, who is al-
ways on the verge of leaving her. She recalls that when she was in Europe
on the trip she made with Jack, her rich uncle had given her a French bond
as a going-away present. This she sells to pay the surgeon. A short time
afterward she becomes pregnant with her son, Hershey. Schwartz makes
much of this; it becomes more than a reminiscence because it calls to mind
one of his major concerns, a theme never long unmentioned in one way or
another in his verse. The first reference to the bond is in the prose, and it
immediately conveys Schwartz's emphasis on the power of the past, the
power of chance, the determined present, the limits of choice.

The prosperity of Eastern European capitalism sent the French
bond west. It went through Paris, the capital of Western culture,

And entered her marriage and entered her womb. (65)

Again the self-consciousness: Schwartz is aware that his degree of interest in such a minor matter is unusual. He knows his obsessions.

> "The sleepless boy has what an oblique mind,
> Thus to have emphasized a minor nut,
> The French bond borne from Bucharest to Brest
> And overseas, over Atlantic rides
> —Surely he might have been born otherwise,
> And what has that to do with what he is?" (66)

What has it to do with what he is, indeed! The man who laid desperate claim to his need for freedom as a defense against the hostile world spent a lifetime of poetry tracking down the accidents that formed his genesis.

> "Forgive the accident of accidents
> Which made you; like the hare-lipped girl,
> Forgive yourself, and like the turning world
> Forgive strange God, maker of Heaven and Earth,
> Who made the spring and fall with a slight tilt. . . ." (67)

Again the god of accident is evoked; the baby is to be named, "announcing the unique inimitable psyche" (69). The act of naming here, as in Schwartz's play *Shenandoah,* sets the child apart, emphasizes for his life his irreducible individuality. Here, for Schwartz, the drama begins and ends in the apparent contradiction or conflict between the freedom of will, which is the prerogative of idiosyncrasy, and the power of circumstance. Eva adored a friend's child, thought him delightful when he smiled and burbled over a piece of Hershey candy. She vowed that she would name her child Hershey, for "looking at him, she saw the image of what she wanted her child to be" (69). And so, deciding in a moment, Baby Green was named Hershey! The third element stressed by the act is the double absurdity—that the significant act of naming should be devolved from a silly whim and that the name decided upon should carry an equally demeaning and silly connotation:

> "The sound which means the ego is alone,
> The bass of harbor boats, alone, alone!
> The pathos of departure's fogbound moan,
> The self's self-exile from the womb and home—"

> "The basis of the art of poetry,
> The hard identity felt in the bone—" (70)

Not as much is made of the matter here as in *Shenandoah* where the naming for which the Jewish religion dictates a special seriousness and a special ritual becomes the core of the play. Where *Shenandoah* achieves some fine poetry with moments of exaltation as well as irony, the poetic comment in *Genesis* falls far short, is, in spots, flat prose, " 'The basis of the art of poetry,' " or stresses the lugubrious, a step below the absurd, and the tone is a shrill jeer.

> "Pigeons pass overhead, and one lets go
> . . . .
> —The one man wet amid the 70,000
> Cries out, Here are 70,000 faces,
> Why did that pigeon have to pick on me?
> —The joke of individuality!" (70)

Or a forced and fake sublimity:

> "—Let us look down from heights, from Everest—"

> "Or from a star, or from Eternity,
> O from Eternity, that is, from Death. . . ." (71)

Appropriately, perhaps, the next episode is the death of Hershey's young uncle, much beloved by Eva. The poetry describes the reaction of Eva, who eyes her child with fear each moment that he, too, might sneeze, catch a cold, and die the way his uncle died, and the reaction of Jack Green, who

> "thinks, not me, not me,
> *him,* but
> Not me! And yet who knows who will be next?
> He says to himself, horrified at heart,
>   facing the first abyss—" (74)

Grubbing unselectively in the cumulus of one's past requires some explanation, especially when it is done publicly and presumably in poetry. One wonders, fairly often, what excuse this poet could give himself for including so much detail in *Genesis*, what motivation beyond mere compulsion could account for the plethora of incident and comment, and, here, in the comment on his uncle's death, Schwartz offers a reason or an excuse. It is needed because the quality of verse in *Genesis* is particularly uneven, and the fault may lie in its unselective quantity. And so, Schwartz writes,

> "This New York boy tells us a piteous story,
> I hear tears in his voice and I hear fear,
> —Calm, calm, poor boy, brimming and obsessed,
> > *Tais-toi,*
> *Pauvre enfant*! endure your past as such:
> No one, not God himself, can learn too much!" (75)

Hershey's first impressive piece of learning involved his position as the center of his mother's love and care. The day after his younger brother's birth Hershey is kept out of his mother's room, something new, with deepest deprivation that no one outgrows. "And thus, faced with this problem, difficulty, and pain, the small mind became creative" (83). This is a reference to an unscientific attitude toward creativity that has ancient antecedents in critical history, that suffering creates art. It may be true that in the discipline there is a curtailing when one wishes to spread and a spreading when one wishes to draw in, which may be the cause of or part of suffering. And, of course, art requires discipline. But it is not necessarily reversible—that discipline or suffering produces art. The "problem, difficulty, and pain" Schwartz mentions may produce actions without strategy (bawling), or feelings (dismay), or actions with strategy such as those entered upon by the wily child who contrives to be taken to the bathroom which, since it is on the other side of his mother's room, naturally allows him to see her. Hershey *was* creative about the strategy; he need not have been; someone else might not have been. If this is the case, then the springs of creativity do not necessarily find their source in suffering. Eva realizes Hershey's cleverness and he is hugged and kissed. But the lesson here for Hershey is not only the joy of cleverness. He has learned to be "alarmed and appalled at the precarious perch of the ego, / And the desperate struggle!" (84).

The nature of his parents is illustrated next in a passage devoted to the naming of Hershey's brother, Roger. Some years before Roger's birth, Jack Green had had an affair with the wife of a streetcar conductor who had a son, Roger. It was the fact of this son that prevailed on her husband to take her back after he learned about the affair from her. She wanted to leave him, but Jack Green rejected her and she went back to her husband. Jack had told Eva about this, and the name "Roger" remained with her associated with her husband's guilt. Without recalling this association, she decided to name her own second born, "Roger." The poetic comment on this is a good example of Schwartz's blank verse; it is like a rickety sled homemade out of modern Tinker-Toy and Erector set parts, cluttered with conceits in the style and analysis in the content, and so burdened with self-conscious colloquialisms (yet both phrase and idea wrapped in timeless pontification) that one wonders what disturbing and not particularly desirable gifts this clumsy Santa will drop off next. It is, nevertheless, persistent and effective.

> "May I psychologize? and thus extend
> —With such a light—all that brimming boy
> Already knows, and mourns? Jack tells his wife,
> Smug and self-satisfied, of an *amour*
> Ten years ago: pleased with himself, in mind
> Too self-pleased, thinking of it, to conceive
> How such a cause must seem to his wife's mind,
> To her mind most of all. There it abides
> With monumental place because it fits
> What interests her the most, Jack's character:
> Cut in her mind as on the continent
> Of North America a glacial age!
> Is this comparison extreme? Behold,
> She names her second son her husband's guilt,
> As self-absorbed, as ignorant as he
> —Each to his blindness through Eternity!"
>
> "Such egoists are so preoccupied
> With their own minds, they lack imagination
> Of what their pride in cleverness must seem
> To someone walking in another dream!"
>
> "Hot tears are sliding down the poor boy's face,
> He sees in all of this identities
> —He would divorce himself from both of them,
> And from himself, a vain and insane hope—" (86–87)

Compare this verse with that of Edwin Arlington Robinson, another modern poet, albeit a generation and a half before Schwartz. Compare it, but not for grading, simply for illumination.

> "I have no more a child,"
> He thought, "and what she is I do not know.
> It may be fancy and fantastic youth
> That ails her now; it may be the sick touch
> Of prophecy concealing disillusion.
> If there were not inwoven so much power
> And poise of sense with all her seeming folly,
> I might assume a concord with her faith
> As that of one elected soon to die." (*Tristram* 41–42)

Both poets are using the line to carry an amount of psychological analysis: Schwartz to show how irrevocably his self-centered parents are separated from each other, neither able to understand the other; Robinson to show the separation of father from daughter where even love supplies no answers and King Howel is left only with conjecture. Schwartz's verse is cacophonous, if not dissonant; one is immediately impressed with the smooth motion of Robinson's. This blank verse, to complement the figure above, would seem like a slick sled dipping down a gentle incline with packages of alliteration and understatement wrapped in high-toned decorum. The strongest contrast lies in the tone: Robinson's is meditative and measured; Schwartz's is overemphatic, almost hysterical. It is as if Robinson's persona is ruminating while Schwartz's is shouting. There is a timelessness about the Robinson diction. The phrasing seems pared down; the texture of modern things whittled off it so that a good part of *Tristram*, really, could have been written, if it were not for some of the close psychological analysis, in an earlier time.

Schwartz shows no regard for the smooth flow, the inhibition, the formal diction; his line contains diverse materials of the times, some pertinent, others peripheral to his immediate theme. It turns back on itself, sometimes more complicated than complex, but usually richer for the tergiversations. It may have a fundamental theme but several themes are kept going at the same time, some at times in opposition to each other. It does not hesitate to move from the formal to the colloquial or the vulgate, from the significant to the trivial. At all times one is conscious of a worldview in process or being manufactured. Robinson writes from within the focus and strength of an established worldview and thus gives the effect of a finished product. Contrast on the level of content nets similar conclusions. Where Schwartz has the burden or the advantage of developed Freudian psychology, Robinson published *Tristram* in 1927, when those insights were just beginning to be available to Americans.

The fact remains, though, that Schwartz's blank verse, perhaps partly because it is so wide open to the invasion of flat realism, is much closer to prose than Robinson's, which falls into dullness where Schwartz's falls into flatness. There is little doubt that Robinson's work is more meticulous, while Schwartz's admits a richer texture. It is not hard to pinpoint the results of Schwartz's willingness to put anything or everything into his line. For instance, just following this passage he writes, "During these years, when the fog of infancy, blooming and booming, slowly lifted" (87). "Booming" is permissible since this brings in the comparison of ships' horns booming in the harbor fog with the noises and voices all around the child. (The real association here, however, comes from William James's "buzzing, booming confusion.") But fog does not "bloom" and the fog Schwartz is describing logically is the opposite of "blooming." So very often this conflict of meaning jams up the line and grinds it to a halt.

The next section of poetic comment anticipates the attempt to merge self with nature that recurs as a significant mode in Schwartz's last poems. Here, in *Genesis*, more than a decade earlier, Schwartz is beginning to use the incantatory phrasing so characteristic of his last poems. He writes about the effect of the snowfall, the joy it gives little Hershey.

> "A game which makes activity pure joy,
> Being itself Being itself, and more
> Than striving for absent future end—" (91)

He seeks to make the identification in an intuited now, the resolution, then, of so much through the mode of mysticism. Here, however, the incantatory repetition defeats itself by the trick of using the verb "being" at the start of the line, thus giving it a spurious capital letter compared to the capitalization of the second "Being." One's attention is attracted to the clever play and distracted from the hypnotic effect that can be developed by such repetition.

Again and again the theme returns to an apology or an explanation for delving into the detail of the past. This time the poet sketches in the image through which the modern American seeks his own significance. He writes first, " '(Europe the greatest thing in North America!' " [96]). And then,

> "Lincoln is on a penny in the mind,
> . . . .
> And Jeeves and Cinderella show the boat
> We all are in, the rotten ship of state!
> Chaplin shuffles and tips his hat! Then runs!
> John Bull and Uncle Sam are not cartoons
> But heavy actual bullies boxing through us!
> They move through all of us, like summer fine:
> Keep thinking all the time, O New York boy!
> Go back,
> In each, all natural being once more lives!" (97)

In all of the passages with this theme, the implication, when it is not stated outright, is that freedom, which seems to be denied to all, may, just may, be achieved by going back, unraveling the threads, learning each link in a chain of cause and effect. Physicists, mathematicians cast probabilities in the twentieth century; with the philosophers they weaken the acceptance of the old notions of cause and effect. But temptation to believe that accident is only accident because the variables are too many for unraveling has been given false authority by a carry-over from psychology that has shown in some areas that there are no accidents. In this passage Schwartz clings to the notion and the attendant ambivalence that had already been expressed many times, one instance being Stephen Crane's "The Blue Hotel." He goes on to give an example of accident and absurdity: Verdi bending down to reach a collar button under the bed, suffering death from apoplexy. The natural corollary is to exalt memory, " 'The memory alone can hold the self!' " (98). And a little farther on, " 'O seek, he means the depths of the Past from which / The soul's moves rise as grasses from the earth—' " (99).

A few lines before this passage is a statement that takes the reader even further back to an earlier verse. In this later line he makes his first thoroughly explicit statement about Hershey's emotional disturbance: " 'In the middle of everything, sick boy' " (99), the speaker addresses Hershey. "Sick boy," the poet writes and one may properly assume he speaks to himself. Earlier occur these lines,

"Hot tears are sliding down the poor boy's face,
He sees in all of this identities
—He would divorce himself from both of them,
And from himself, a vain and insane hope—" (87)

The memory in its tireless seeking, just as is promised by the hope of psychoanalysis, ferrets out the earliest traumas, admits them, examines them. But even Freud was not too successful in his attempt at self-analysis. Perhaps the poet has no clinical intentions; perhaps he does this, as he openly avows, to clarify and to understand and with the hope of perfecting his will. What is more touching than the need to reject both parents in their totality? What is more extreme in the young than the denial of self that Schwartz admits is "a vain and insane hope"? Already, the young boy watches himself; if he cannot change altogether, then he can at least weed out part of himself; but he must stay aware, awake, and on the defensive— the beginning of the poet's supernally active self-consciousness!

In the very next prose section, he is unjustly accused by the teacher, and when she, nevertheless, approaches him in his exile outside the school room to comfort him, he feels

the wish to cry and the wish to suppress emotion,
The wish to howl his cause, and yet the wish to get the kind-
ness and not cry:
He tried, he turned his face away, the kindness was too much,
He burst into tears! helpless with grief and self-pity, already
the actor and the victim of what a constellation of emotions,
Injustice, paranoia, bursting tears, and most of all, deliberate
withdrawal to show his strength and pride—
Already active in the fifth year; for this was the beginning of
his childhood. (101)

Almost at the same time, another element of disturbance was being prepared. He loses his fountain pen and tells his mother, asking her not to tell his father. But when he goes to bed his father asks him where his pen is. Hershey begins to lie. Jack Green smiles broadly and proffers his own pen, pays no attention to Hershey's lie. Hershey is overjoyed at the same moment that a shadow of distrust engulfs him. His mother has betrayed him.

"—The sense that always underneath the face
Many a motive hid the truth, prepared

Illusions, made the mirage, deceived!"

"Life is a lie! Life is a long long lie. . . ." (105)

Thus far a genesis is traced from rejection of his parents to rejection of himself to a split marked by victim and actor in the drama he also watches, and, finally, the great betrayal. Again, explicitly, he names his early self-consciousness. He adds:

> "My fear is light, narcissist interest
> Engages me, as if I played a game—
> A game of tennis, close, hotly contested
> —Yet, at the same time, gazed from the grandstand,
>   cool!" (111)

And here also Hershey gives an argument for avoiding choice. This argument, or perhaps rationalization, is associated in part with Schwartz's "life-style," an emphatic and continuous incorporation. It is Schwartz whose lines show this incorporative mode, but it is the person, Hershey, in *Genesis,* who is given this comment.

> "Choice cuts the heart in half as the lungs breathe,
> Those ultimate balloons! Choice cuts the heart
> In half and throws away one half as if
> The unelected half were useless rind!" (111)

And the alternative to choice is not to choose at all, but it is to choose both, to consume both alternatives so they are alternatives no longer. It is, certainly, not an intellectual choice but an emotional one.

The analysis continues; the hope, then, is that the watcher who watches sensitively and completely will be other than the one who is watched. The slight transcendence momentarily achieved is intellectual not existential. The poet tells the story of his attempt to get into the bathroom whence a pretty lady friend of his mother's has retired, because he felt that inside there she was naked and he wanted to see her naked.

> Until grandmother drew him away, saying, Shame on you!
>   Shame on you!
>   The far-off cries of the Super-ego! (115)

Such heavy-handed interpolation of clinical jargon cannot help being ruinous to the poetry. But it is not this language alone that accounts for th grossness of many lines. Another sententious line is, " 'The War again Cain's everlasting sin. . . .' " (108). It is the need of the poet to bring hi culture images into bas-relief, so to speak, at every opportunity. Unsur about his images—not what they are but what claims they have on th other person, on the reader (because he suspected himself of being, in a way, a monster)—he finds it necessary to buttress them with intellectual ized images, all built from a blueprint of logical argument. This intrusior into the poetry sometimes works, sometimes is devastating. Nevertheless it should be pointed out that such passages as the following have a specia importance:

> "When I looked down at Life for the first time,
> It was as if I turned to the comic strips,
>
> . . . .
> Unlikely slots and strips of comedy,
> Speaking balloons! as if they did not live,
> Had not true being (somewhat Platonic then
> My frame of mind). But, as the clown slid on,
> Perceived the universals in the art,
> Saw Jiggs as Everyman and Jiggs' wife
> As the harsh criticism Everyman endures,
> No hero to his wife: at least, that is,
> In lower-middle-class America,
> Among the Joneses rising in the world,
> Among that Mutt and Jeff, or Sancho Panza
> And Don Quixote, deathless in this life—" (134)

The images in the culture of America, like Jung's archetypes, come from the deeps of consciousness, rise and instruct as Schwartz repetitively teaches. It is worth noting that in a great many, almost a majority, of the reports of "trips" taken under psychedelic drugs, significant encounters are made with cartoon characters, some of which are the standard ones engraved on the mass mind, others cartooned or caricatured representations of children or adults known by the subject of new "friends," who, nevertheless, take on this exaggerated and satirical nature. What it comes down to in such cases is the manufacturing of a cosmic joke, heavy-handed and overstated like many of Schwartz's representations. In fact, the Freudian divisions of

the personality—Ego, Id, and Super-Ego—after a time become more than
imaginative tools in a methodology and take on the body and size of mytho-
poetic images.

> "The Id or daemon sleeps like a great river,
> On it the ego, rowing back and forth—" (141)

More of the poetic content is taken away from the great ghosts, and it is
given to Hershey to speak—the older Hershey. Thus, the identification
with the author, Schwartz, becomes more open as the work draws to con-
clusion. Events from the childhood of Hershey are described and explained
over and over. Those chosen are crucial and no nuance of action or under-
standing escapes the analysis of the poet. Nevertheless, little of the fresh-
ness of childhood is conveyed in the poetry. It is mentioned, described,
discussed but always by the ghosts or by the older Hershey. There is more,
really, of a child's wonder and vision in the poem " 'I Am Cherry Alive,'
the Little Girl Sang" in *Summer Knowledge* than in the whole of *Genesis*.
It is the hand of Hershey but the voice of Schwartz, as it were.

The marriage, unhappy and doomed, rocks on, and one sees the suffer-
ing laid on Hershey by the battling parents, who, in Schwartz's eyes, are
too self-centered to notice. Yet the child assumes the parents' way, particu-
larly that of his father, who

> Could not hold down the paranoiac ego, prepared to believe
> that all, in the secret incestuous adulterous heart he knew him-
> self,
> Enacted Iago, Brutus, Judas, Clytemnestra, Delilah, or
> Gertrude,
> Always betraying him! (148)

His father leaves, finally, and divorce action is in the making. Eva re-
fuses to move out of the comfortable house until Jack promises that, if she
lets him sell it at a profit, he will come back home again. He moves them
all into a cheap apartment and leaves. Even little Hershey feels the depri-
vation and the betrayal. Now he realizes his individuality:

> "The middle-class delights are not for you,
> The handsome furniture, the set of silver, . . .
> . . . .

> —For you belong with us, remorse's troops,
> Gaining through pain and through unhappiness,
> Knowledge, freedom, hope, forgiveness, love!" (176–77)

And so his childhood ended. The scene recalled is " 'The husband trapped while dining with a whore' " (205). Eva, with little Hershey in hand, finds her husband at a table in the fine restaurant of a roadhouse; she stands and loudly berates him. He walks out with the child, lights a cigarette. And Hershey "admired most of all his father's poise and dignity, after Medea cried aloud and Clytemnestra struck!" (205). The comment states explicitly:

> "Childhood was ended here! or innocence
> —Henceforth suspicious of experience!" (206)

The end of *Genesis* approaches; it rises like a fountain. Hershey's hope crashes on the hard rock of cynicism (which he learned from his father was intelligence!), and, finally, it rises again at the very end. First, he does not know, cannot tell, that " 'Everything happens in the mind of God' " (208). Actually,

> "This hideous scene presents the biggest truth,
> Man's Nature is this being-in-the-world,
> This in-ness is the warmest thing in Life,
> This in-ness is the widest thing in Life,
> This is the space in which you live your Life!" (206)

Here is stated the insight that became Schwartz's final fundamental theme running through all of his last poems. This is what one *has*, the only illumination, the only place to explore, the only means by which one *can* explore. In "Dr. Bergen's Belief," Dr. Bergen insists that his insights must face the final, full perspective of death, and he leaps from a building to prove the value of this perspective. In *Genesis*, published when Schwartz was thirty, this hope rises like an organ note in this last lines:

> "*O what a metaphysical victory*
> *The first morning and night of death must be!*" (208)

MIDDLE POEMS 1948–1950

VAUDEVILLE FOR A PRINCESS

In *Vaudeville for a Princess*, Delmore Schwartz's "middle poems," he abandons much of the personal preoccupation, the great weight of youthful insight that had to be expressed in his early work. The same matters still affect him and demand expression, but he is now looking at their surface. He is turning outward for an examination of society in pretty much its own terms, and his style is surer, speedier, even slicker.

The first section is a statement of Schwartz's sensitivity to the absurd. In the first poem, "On a Sentence by Pascal," Pascal is quoted, " 'True eloquence mocks eloquence,' " and Schwartz wishes to know,

> Did that Frenchman mean
> That heroes are hilarious
> And orators obscene? (3)

He ends the short poem,

> And smiles, being meticulous,
> Because truth is ridiculous. (3)

The entire section is composed in the same fashion as "Coriolanus and His Mother," only without the plot development: short poems interspersed with prose vignettes airing Schwartz's opinions on existentialism, Hamlet, Othello, driving automobiles, and the social responses of a "great poet." What ties it together is the implication of the absurd and a statement that is sarcastic, cynical, or satirical, as the case may be—a recital of one disenchantment after another. It was all very well for the clear-eyed, strong-voiced young man to have written so insightfully about the perpetual lack of solace in "The Repetitive Heart," but here the poet shows that, as an older man, he faces the same dismaying insights but with the acerbity of greater commitment. In this book, in several poems where he forgets to save himself by the comic frame, he is on his way to a carping bitterness. Eventually, as in his last poems, he develops a mode of salvation in which all disappointments together with all contradictions are resolved by a massive affirmation: "And yet through all these mounting fears / How I am glad that I exist!" (14).

The estate of poets is considered. "True Recognition Often Is Refused" begins, "We poets by the past and future used," and ends:

> For we must earn through dull dim suffering,
> Through ignorance and darkened hope, and hope
> Risen again, and clouded over again, and dead
> despair. . . . (20)

But Schwartz has a stronger point to make. The tone without the affirmation is a whine, but splendid affirmation saves both this bad poem and another poem in this section, "The Masters of the Heart Touched the Unknown." Here Schwartz, on a note of high appreciation, exploits two themes that are found in his work from the beginning: his appreciation for his cultural heroes, and his respect for the powerful effort they made (and therefore each of us should make) toward self-knowledge. It is no accident that Socrates is Schwartz's first and last hero. After citing the passionate culmination of Keats, Oscar Wilde, Mozart, Victor Hugo, Baudelaire, Emily Brontë, Henry James, Wordsworth, and Dostoevsky, he sums up:

> These masters used their lives like Christmas trees,
> They skinned themselves alive to find the truth,
> They gazed upon their vileness like excrement.
> They ate their hearts to sate the need for love.
> They fingered every coiled snake of the mind. . . .
>   (35)

Part II consists of eight poems cast in this new mold. Sarcasm, rather than irony, persists. Each poem is introduced by "Dear Citizens," whom he neither loves nor considers enfranchised, and it is here that a shift in perspective becomes obvious. These poems truly constitute a bridge between his first poems and his last. They look backward to his early poetry in that they are iambic pentameter dialogues with himself, the old arguing-out of the problem, the setting forth of first one side then the other so that the whole is finally illuminated. The section is titled "The True, The Good, and The Beautiful" and contains eight poems in which Schwartz puts himself under third degree for moral and motive examination—the "heavy bear" as against the ideal self—with reality not as the reward but as the punishment. These poems in their interlacing themes, the claims and counter-claims, the occasional refrain, the accent on degradation, absurdity, and despair are reminiscent of the eleven terrifying philosophical poems in the section called "The Repetitive Heart" in his first book. In both sets of poems, solace (the good, the true, and the beautiful) is lost almost irretrievably, in each case, except for a desperate, romantic affirmation. In the early poetry the accent of the affirmation is on the real; it is on love and companionship, more the latter than the former:

> When we are in step, running together,
> Our pace equal, our motion one,
> Then we will be well, parallel and equal,
>
> . . . .
> Moving together through time to all good.
> (*In Dreams Begin Responsibilities* 104)

In the later poems of *Vaudeville for a Princess*, the object of the affirmation is more tenuous, more on the side of the ideal. It is, in fact, the Socrates-Platonic imperative, "Know thyself." The last line of the imperative in this section is "What is our hope, except to tell the truth?" (63). This is followed by the emphasis on the good, the true, and the beautiful. It can be contended that Schwartz has buried these abstractions under a mire of savagery, absurdity, and horror and that they emerge, if at all, dripping with cynicism and despair. They do emerge, nevertheless, and as signals of an irrepressible urge in the author and, by implication, in humans. Thus, the affirmation here leans toward the abstract, points in the direction of Schwartz's last poems. In these it is more tenuous, even though at the heart of the celebration of the physical world, and it moves to the last resort, the affirmation of affirmation itself.

Another, subtler change stems probably from the greater maturity of the poet. A quieter, surer line develops. It shows all the assets of the professional and also some of the liabilities as, for example, it provides greater breadth and variety of texture but neither digs as freshly nor explodes as sharply as the earlier verse. The cause lies, it seems, in the acceptance of certain common verbal counters that young poets, in their zeal to keep stereotypes out of their poetry, urgently strive to avoid. The more mature poet, accepting the necessity of working with words, most of which are well-thumbed counters, turns the conventional combinations to his own advantage. Their use makes it possible to widen the field of comment and to speed and weight the conclusions. Where, formerly, Schwartz would have been avid to convey, in image and symbol, every experimental nuance of the kinds of heartache, he now uses the general statement to cover it in one line, " 'And of the evil native to the heart' " (53). Or he says, " 'I am a pupil of emotion's wrongs / Performed upon the glory of this world' "(53).

In his earlier poetry he listed each of the wrongs, communicated the feeling of them, the intense and intimate struggle. Before, he was inside; now, he is beyond that, outside, and is able to talk *about* these matters, to make a summing up. This further stage may have a tendency to produce prosier lines, for there is almost as much discourse as there is presentation, but his rhythm, density, and control prevent this from occurring. Instead of presenting the original struggle, he is now making conclusions. Slightly removed from the experience, older and wiser in the experiencing, he has the right to look up from his personal agonies, set them in their place in society, and sum it all up.

In each of the first poems of this set, Schwartz offers first a condemnation of the world and his position in it and then justification for it or for himself. Since the circumstance is an extreme contradiction of the true, the good, and the beautiful, Schwartz's rejoinders, although truthful and honest, mock themselves in their comparative weakness and rely for their opposing weapon only on the fact of the poetry itself. This fact implies an insistence, a stubbornness, and a gallantry that are the author's ultimate stance and that, it is implied, ought to be ours as well. In a way, this is Schwartz's answer to Eliot's "After such knowledge, what forgiveness?" (30).

The first poem is titled "He Heard the Newsboys Shouting 'Europe! Europe!' " (53). He has been excused from the war and feels called upon to justify himself. He asks:

> "What have I done which is a little good?
> What apples have I grasped, for all my years?
> What starlight have I glimpsed for all my guilt?" (53)

In the face of the Holocaust, all he can reply is that he is a poet, " 'a student of the morning light, / . . . a pupil of emotion's wrongs' " (53), and he adds that he has dedicated himself to the true, the good, and the beautiful.

The second poem, "The Silence Answered Him Accusingly," continues: " 'Don't tell yourself a noble lie once more!' " (54). And now, he merely adds the fact that he is also a teacher and teaches the young about the true, the good, and the beautiful. He ends the poem with " ' "Plato's starlight glitters amid the shocking wars" ' " (54). The third poem is named "Such Answers Are Cold Comfort to the Dead." It points out that he teaches for money while other boys are " 'slumped like sacks on desperate shores' " (55). He again makes his innocent plea for " 'the kinds of light,' " for the " 'wakeful night,' " " 'unknown America,' " and " 'love's long defeat,' " and closes with the gentle, " 'May I not cite this as a little good?' " (55).

A recital of the vulgar joys of the playground, Luna Park, in Coney Island, follows, but it is not the vulgarity that is uncovered but the unconscious, the secret areas that find their satisfaction in such a circus. This is, of course, an uncovering of us all, and we are meant to see ourselves according to his vision. Although we all are condemned, it must not be forgotten that his, before all, is *his* vision. He ends the poem relentlessly:

> This is the Luna of the heart's desire,
> This is the play and park we all admire. (59)

Of the last four poems, two end in despair and two with a hope that mocks hope: "What is our hope, except to tell the truth?" (63) and "What but with patient hope to try again?" (61). The poem "Most Things at Second Hand Through Gloves We Touch" ends:

> *Duncan is dead, and Desdemona, innocent,*
> *Is choked to death. The true, the good,*
> *And the beautiful have been struck down*
> *Because of what they are. No matter what you say,*
> *This is not brushed away. No matter what you say,*
> *This is the way it is, year by year and day by day.* (62)

Here, then, in his mid-thirties, the poet has taken inventory. He is no longer seeking himself. He knows who he is and it has, for the moment, brought him peace and allowed him some fine verse. The poetry does not have the impact of the earlier work, but it possesses a new authority. It is more complete, more sophisticated. Schwartz has become a man of the world, a man of the poetic world. And, in poetry, the pain of experience seems no longer so immediate. Good is destroyed perpetually by evil, truth distorted by desire, and beauty blinded by vulgarity. What is left is to try again and again, to hope to tell the truth, and to love. In his attempt to embrace the present reality, Schwartz is left with these imperatives. The last one, love, leads into the third section of the book, which is titled "The Early Morning Light."

For Schwartz the morning, the early morning, has always constituted a rebirth, a symbol of awakening, of freshness, of renewal: "the travail / Of early morning, the mystery of beginning / Again and again" (*In Dreams Begin Responsibilities* 134). A quotation is affixed beneath the title. It is from F. Scott Fitzgerald, "In the real dark night of the soul, it is always three o'clock in the morning" (65). There is hope, the quotation implies, and it is followed by a group of forty love sonnets. With this, the structure of the book becomes clear. The sonnets are to Elizabeth Follet, who became the poet's wife for a time, and the book is called *Vaudeville for a Princess*. Thus, the first section of the book elaborates the disappointments of the rational man in the absurd universe; the second section the horror of the good man at the evil in society; and the third section the salvation by love which is coupled with beauty. Taken in order, this covers the true, the good, and the beautiful and is an appropriate vaudeville for the poet's true princess, Elizabeth (Follet), to whom it is appropriately dedicated. The elaborate pun is also contributed to by the fact that Schwartz conceived of himself, especially in connection with his beloved, as a clown or a "heavy bear," and this marks, of course, the distance between Princess Elizabeth and Danny Kaye.

The third section contains forty poems, thirty-five of which are sonnets or near sonnets. These are constructed with rigor, the area weakest in conformity and widest in possibility being the rhyme. Here Schwartz allows himself greater latitude than in the sonnets he published in *In Dreams Begin Responsibilities*. Here almost any combination of rhyme scheme may be found, and sometimes a line forgets to rhyme at all or never intended to. The remaining five poems (86, 87, 90, 91, and 92), which do not approach the sonnet structure, are simply separate variations. "Twelfth Night, Next Year, a Week-end in Eternity" seems to be a blowup or gaseous sonnet. It has fourteen lines and a ragged rhyme scheme that is a lumbering approximation of the sonnet, but the meter is so loose and, in cases, muddles down into a prose rhythm so heavy that one hesitates to assign it to this classification. It has, in fact, signs of structural loosening, which point to the loosening of Schwartz's line in his last poetry. It shows the lengthening of the line, the flat, prosy statement, and possibly, for the first time, the opening of a line to mystical apprehension through hypnotic repetition: "And listening and silent, and silent and listening, and listening and silent" (90).

Although this section is titled "The Early Morning Light" which, as was indicated, is a repeated and legitimate symbol Schwartz uses for renewal, rebirth, and hope, these themes assert themselves against a miasma of cynicism and despair. Certainly the power of enthusiasm, hope, and joy in some of the lines is often able to counteract the great negations that usually precede or follow them. These sonnets, celebrating his relationship with the young woman who became his second wife, seldom contain living space for joy untainted by self-conscious self-deprecation or by cynicism and doubt or by hopeless assessments of the poet's place in modern society. America is examined, accepted, and rejected. Modern success, eyed askance, turns out to be failure. Yet the poet deplores his inability to achieve it. Even the relationship he has with his beloved is exposed in its limitations, all of his fears and timidities ruthlessly illumined.

To examine the last theme first, one need only look at the final lines in the two sonnets that face each other on the pages; these are the sixth and seventh in the series. The sixth is called "The Self-Betrayal Which Is Nothing New" and the seventh sonnet is called "I Wish I Had Great Knowledge or Great Art." Given in order, the last two lines are "The one who wants to know her endlessly" (72) and "Two worlds are separated endlessly" (73). Here is a terrible and romantic circumstance where the deepest need is met by the bitterest opposition. These lines constitute the twin classifications under which the thematic material of the sonnets may be listed: the enthusiastic and joyous moments in the class of the deepest need, and the doubts and denigrations in the class of denial; the former his wanting "to know her endlessly," and the latter "two worlds" that are "separated endlessly."

Representations of these two themes intertwine in most of the sonnets. Only seldom does a sonnet offer one alone. Examining "The Self-Betrayal Which Is Nothing New," one sees another facet of the same problem. In the very moment that leads the poet to declare his endless need for his lover, he also shows the dilemma of having to become, in order to be "most prosperous for her," the very being that could never need her "endlessly":

> what can I do
> To make myself most prosperous for her?
> I asked myself, conjuring dignities:
> Bestseller book or hit upon Broadway,
> All of the limelight's bright banalities,
> Hurried to Hollywood and a photoplay,
>
> Or a high chair in the old academies? (72)

And he concludes that he is in the deplorable situation just outlined:

> Lucky or strong, I can get everything
> But what I want the most! For having these,
> I would be but a matinée's false king,
> For in that glare and gilt, I would not be
> The one who wants to know her endlessly. (72)

There is no doubt that frequently the Schwartz poem comes in like a lion—and fails to maintain its initial strength. That the failure is just as frequently good poetry regardless of the fact that it is not up to the opening is another matter. Sometimes, however, the poem dissipates as it moves on and finally is unrealized.

The first sonnet in this section, "The Winter Twilight, Glowing Black and Gold," opens magnificently. In the first stanza, Schwartz produces a brilliant image to convey at what stage he is in life:

> That time of year you may in me behold
> When Christmas trees are blazing on the walk,
> Raging amid stale snow against the cold
> And low sky's bundled wash, senseless as chalk. (67)

Characteristically, he makes use of the adjusted quotation, much as Eliot did before him. Thus, the reader begins the poem hearing overtones of Shakespeare and Eliot, moves on to a second line reminiscent of Allen Tate's "Sonnets at Christmas," touches in the fifth line a chord from Hart Crane, in "Hissing and ravenous the brilliant plant, / Rising like eagerness" (67), moves on to a note from Auden in the second stanza, "But this is only true at four o'clock, / At noon the fifth year is once more abused" (67), and ends, finally, with a Schwartzian emphasis:

> I bring a distant girl apples and cake,
> Pictures, secrets, lastly my swollen heart,
> Now boxed and tied by what I know of art
> —But as before accepted and refused. (67)

This is not only what it states explicitly, that the poet offers his affirmation, his bursting enthusiasm to a girl and all that he proffers is accepted, then refused. Schwartz is also saying that the ambivalence he encountered from one he admired at four years old is repeated when he again, as an adult, offers a girl his heart, but he also makes reference to his heart being "boxed and tied by what I know of art." What has he to add, as an adult, is his poetry; he has a new loyalty. And could it be that his offering in meter receives from those it is bestowed upon precisely the same acceptance and refusal accorded his person years before?

The second stanza is prosy, flat, and colorless. This is a falling off from the rhetoric of the first stanza, as if the weariness of the rejection entered finally into the poetic line itself where it does not have to be. It promises at the beginning to be a poem of the persona's rejection, not the poet's impotence. Compared with many other of the sonnets, this is, nevertheless, a good poem. A large percentage of the others fall off just as this one, but they fall farther and flatter.

Not all the sonnets are love poems. Some mark a sad apex of sobriety, the moment when a glance, unfueled by feeling, reveals the gray world of an enervated poet. The vibrancy of discovery is gone; the early rage and protest are gone. What of the "early morning light"? Schwartz finds most appropriate "the oyster light of the wool sky," and he asks, "Is this not, after all, appropriate / Light for a long used poet such as I?" (91). The poet still sounds his challenges, but they seem like familiar gestures without the persuasion of power. He asserts that there is a Santa Claus but "his hands are dirty, his fingers inkstained, and his arms weak," and he issues his promise, referring to Santa Claus as "A sad clown in polka gown whom my applause / Will once more invigorate, before the coming wars" (90). It is as if the initial attack has petered out. The cavalry of rationality, the poniards and lances of the Cartesian culture have been blunted with use, while the enemy, having absorbed all possible punishment, looms just as formidable on a horizon that creeps closer and closer.

What has happened, put another way, is this: the real and ideal seem just as separated, just as irreconcilable as they ever were, no matter how strong the poet's assertions to the contrary. They are precisely as far apart as, through the power of his position defined by his culture heroes, he has insisted on keeping the subjective and the objective apart. He is at the point where he has worn out his world. He is on the verge of impassivity, apathy, paralysis. In brief, he has taught himself to go with the red light and stop with the green, and he has seen, for some time, that *both* are burning brightly. It is, in fact, salvation that he is going to have to seek, both as a poet and a man, and this will involve an ability, somehow, to get himself out of the dilemma of intrinsic separation—stylistically, philosophically, and emotionally.

LAST POEMS 1959–1961

Summer Knowledge

Delmore Schwartz, like everyone else, was the hero of his own dreams, and these were dreams of affirmation. The subtitle to the first of the two main divisions of his last book *Summer Knowledge: New and Selected Poems 1938–1958,* "The Dreams Which Begin in Responsibilities," is a reversal of the title of his first book, and this new title refers to the same early poems that were among the first he published. Part two, which is headed "Summer Knowledge," has five subsections: "The Fulfillment," "Morning Bells," "The Kingdom of Poetry," "The Deceptive Present, The Phoenix Year," and "The Phoenix Choir."

The perfect titles tell the story. They are a questioning, a gathering together of judgments and insights, an exorcism, a celebration of life, and a seeking of reinforcement, of assent, in the lives of others. Schwartz seems to know that the chips are down, that he has reached the end of "incorporation," that poetry and protest can only do so much. Surrounded by the closed system of human limitation, he has scoured the inside surface for ways out. Now he is thrown back, as are all people, on what has been given from the first. If he cannot actually transcend this, he will at least act out transcendence symbolically and, if nothing else, at least heroism and beauty will sputter against the darkness. The *summarium in excelsis* begins. One is tempted to quote Wallace Stevens from "Puella Parvula":

> Hear what he says,
> The dauntless master, as he starts the human tale. (456)

Schwartz begins with the open admission of ritual. "At a Solemn Musick" borrows Teutonic gravity and pomp by its spelling. As usual, he is protectively mocking. Let us have a ritual of chant and song, he is saying, and let it be a grave admission of limitation and a celebration of the true and only power. Each stanza begins with instructions to the musicians and singers. "Now may the chief musician say" (147) is the first of these. The poem traces life in the world where " '*Lust and emulation . . . / Have inhabited our hearts . . . and ravished / The substance of pity and compassion*' " (147).

But the quotidian is perpetually redeemed by " '*The river of the morning . . . / [that flows] out of the splendor of the tenderness of surrender*' " (147). One recalls that morning is always the fresh beginning. Then occurs a key sentence, " '*Nothing is more important than summer*' " (147). This associates the title of the book and carries a faint overtone of the word "knowledge," but it is followed by a question mark. It is answered in this fashion: Schwartz brings up the great question of death as if to ask what knowledge or even "summer knowledge" can have to say about this, and then gives the first reply:

> "*The phoenix is the meaning of the fruit,*
> *Until the dream is knowledge and knowledge is a dream.*" (147)

He describes the choir as "Ascending and descending the heights of assent" (148). At the end of the poem, he gives his final answer, although not in its fullest form; later his answer is developed and built upon. This is addressed to "love and love's victory" (147), love being the strongest affirmation, the opposite to self:

> *Before the morning was, you were:*
> *Before the snow shone,*
> *And the light sang, and the stone,*
> *Abiding, rode the fullness or endured the emptiness,*
> *You were: you were alone.* (148)

But self is what Schwartz's poetry is about. It is self and selfhood that to this point have always been affirmed, if only between the lines. The poet knows that his salvation lies in another direction. He is his own medicine man, concocting beautiful spells in which he does not wholly believe. In other words, the integrity is in the poem as exorcism, as a legitimate expression, but the real-life effectiveness of the chosen means is doubted, it seems, by Schwartz and also, somehow, by the reader.

"The Fulfillment," the third poem in this section, continues the dialectic. The poet has already brought up the question of knowledge. Although he returns to it later, now he takes up "the dream." The poem sets up an imagined point of transcendency, an afterlife, as it were, from which this life is evaluated. Schwartz writes bitterly of the frequency with which he was admonished,

" 'Beware of all your desires. You are deceived.
(As they are deceived and deceptive, urgent and passing!' " (150)

With such an admonition go the great promises of the City of God, given in the first half of each of the following two lines. But in the second half is that part of the statement that, in a sense, Schwartz takes over in a change of tone. The terseness and repetition bespeak a bitterness that is the poet's, not the promiser's:

" 'They will be wholly fulfilled. You will be dead.
They will be gratified. And you will be dead.' " (150)

The poet pictures himself in just such a circumstance where, giving all credit due, "all things existed purely in the action of joy— / . . . only as the structures of joy!" (150). Then he adds, "It was then that we saw what was lost as we knew where we had been" (150). Here the reader is brought to the first step of the celebration of living. The drama of his statement gains through contrast with the device of the imagined transcendency.

And knew for the first time the richness and poverty
Of what we had been before and were no more,
The striving, the suffering, the dear dark hooded morality. . . .
(150–51)

The fulfillment of the old expectation is not fulfillment. There is either no fulfillment or it lies in the world, and the richness (and the poverty) of existence is not only dramatically unveiled at the end of the last stanza, but with it, in tone, a tragic longing for the world, a treasuring of the things in it, that can come only from one who knew them once but can never know them again.

The last two poems in this section are of special significance. No other poems in the remaining sections have the centrality, or the success, of these. One is a prayer, the other a celebration, and together they constitute as complex a meditation as any one of the four quartets of Eliot. "The First Morning of the Second World" picks up where "The Fulfillment" leaves off. The second world is the world of Lazarus when he returns. The lost soul of "The Fulfillment" has returned to the world, sees it fresh and new. The poet in another sense is being twice-born: the transcendency is not just a device any longer; it is an accomplished fact. The breakthrough *is* a breakthrough into love and, momentarily, out of the bonds of self. Schwartz accurately pictures himself at the beginning of the poem,

> locked
> And intent in that vigil in which the hunter is hunted
> As the mind is, seeking itself, falconer, falcon and hawk,
> victor and victim. . . . (152)

What he pictures next is, perhaps, not so much a breakthrough as a breaking. At base only hostility and fear could build the network of armament used for his protection: the play at the role of the clown, the irony, the occasional smart-alec sophistication. Although none of this clouded the honesty of his work, it produced countless feints and divagations, moues, and it set the tone of struggle, sadness, and disappointment. Now comes the statement of release in what he refers to in the poem "At a Solemn Musick" as " '*the tenderness of surrender*' " (147). Compassion is aroused when he describes the situation: "The gun of the mind ached in my numb and narrowed gaze" (152). His mind with its insistence on a special and respected kind of wholeness, his former style with its reliance on the logical enterprise once called "tension" by Allen Tate, could no longer maintain the same old coping. The moment is at hand when a widening of his concept of knowledge must occur and when the style must loosen to contain it.

> Certainly and suddenly, for a moment's eternity, it was the
> ecstasy and stillness of the white
> wizard blizzard, the white god fallen, united,
> entirely whiteness
> The color of forgiveness, beginning and hope. (152)

The next stanza continues the experience, builds a holiday of whiteness and takes him into memory. He is moving from the general, the abstract (he has already called anger abstract) to the particular, divesting himself of hostility.

> —How could I have known that the years and the hopes were
> human beings hated or loved, . . .
> . . . .
> There they were, all of them, and I was with them,

They were with me, and they were me, I was them, forever united
As we all moved forward in a consonance silent and moving
   Seated and gazing,
     Upon the beautiful river forever. (153)

In part two of the poem, he begins the identification of love with knowledge that will find its fullest resolution in the poem "Summer Knowledge": "There is nothing to think but drink of love and knowledge, and love's knowledge" (153). He admits that he is dropping his defenses: "and no more masks or unmasking" (153). His surrender goes even further; he refers to "thought's abdication" that "quickens thought's exultation" (153) and "My lips trembled, fumbled, and in the depths and *death of thought*" (154; italics added). The sharp differentiations of words blur in the process of repetition and ritual. Acuteness of thought dissolves in the attempt to contain, control, and communicate the uncontrollable swell of feeling and insight.

Suddenly and certainly I saw how surely the measure and
   treasure of pleasure is being as being with, belonging
Figured and touched in the experience of voices in chorus.
     Withness is ripeness,
     Ripeness is withness,
     To be is to be in love,
       Love is fullness of being. (154)

One can only betray the experience in attempting to communicate it, especially in exposition, yet the attempt should be made. Part 3 begins with a rapturous description of the encounter with this experience of love. What is felt, in part, is possibly the ecstasy of relieving oneself of the burden of self, a burden unseemly heavy for a poet who turned, twisted, probed, and scarred himself decade after decade. The second stanza of Part 3 begins "Suddenly, suddenly and certainly" (155). The repetition of "certainly" in the poem is in its context almost a refrain. The joys of certitude are surely appreciated by a man who has had to maintain the tension of provisionality all his life. He emphasizes the freshness of the moment and, finally, arrives, toward the end of the poem, at the great final identification of love and renewed life. This is a moment of tremendous and fresh experience for the poet. It promises rebirth, even eternal life, in a special sense, and Schwartz, seeking to give the experience its fullest rendering, compares it to the discovery of the second world by Lazarus. Only a complete quotation of this ending can supply the immense reaches of excitement, the astonishing, rich organ note that rises, with more complexity if less rhetoric than the ending of Dylan Thomas' poem "Ceremony After a Fire Raid":

> Quickly and certainly it was the little moment when Lazarus
> Thrusting aside the cold sweated linens,
> Summoned by Jesus, snow and morning,
> Thrust the stone to the side, the fell conclusion,
> And knew all astonishment for the first time, wonderstruck
> *Not* that he lived again, after the wood, the stone, the closing,
>   nails, and black silence empty,
> But that he had ever died. Knew the illusion of death confused
>   with the reality of the agony of dying,
> Knowing at last that death is inconceivable among the living
> (Knowing the wish, the hope, the will, the luxury and
>   ignorance of the thought that man can ever die)
> Hearing the thunder of the news of waking from the false
>   dream of life that life can ever end. (155–56)

Although Schwartz was not "Summoned by Jesus," he was summoned by the snow and the morning—the call to renascence—as he points out in the second line above.

"Summer Knowledge," which follows, seeks to convey the experience of the kind of knowledge that Schwartz is substituting for the mixture of closed systems—concepts and values—that have held his loyalty to this point. If there is a new difference, it is in insight and feeling. It appears to be a spontaneous, mystical acceptance that yields an enriched and exultant perceptivity.

> Summer knowledge is not picture knowledge, nor is it the
>   knowledge of lore and learning.
> . . . .
> For summer knowledge is the knowledge of death as birth,
> . . . .
> For, in a way, summer knowledge is not knowledge at all: it is
>   second nature, first nature fulfilled, a new birth
> . . . .
> In the consummation and the annihilation of the blaze of fall.
>   (157)

The temptation is to continue to transfer as much of this material to the expository level as possible. This is not only because the material is fascinating but because it seems too possible to do it. Now these are not the usual characteristics of mystical experience. Such experience is supposed to be ineffable. It should be, by and large, beyond the communicative power of words. In truth, it does result here in an unusual amount of paradox per linear inch, but the possibility of successfully discoursing on it looms large. It may be because Schwartz himself is providing the discourse. Although he is writing poetry, if only because of the sublimity, it is a peculiar poetry, very close to discussion, to discourse, to prose. He is talking too much *about* his subject; he is not rendering it excellently enough. For many obvious reasons it is fair to say that his goal is more than discussion, and it is fair, then, to conclude that his means are not up to his ends. This is a failure in style brought about by his inability to foreshorten his focus on his material, while at the same time, he sought to communicate intimately. There was a time when this approach was equal to intimate communication; the paradoxes of St. John of the Cross are a good example. But they will not do for now—incorporated into a poem by Eliot, or separately on their own— any more than Schwartz's will do for him and for now. Schwartz moved inward in vision and outward in style when he should have taken the direction of a Rimbaud, Crane, or Ashbery.

The material just considered is central; the other poems in this section of "Summer Knowledge" are corollary or decorative. The group titled "Morning Bells" contains just what its title implies, lyrics (six of them) of a fresh and positive nature. Only one calls for special attention: the lovely song " 'I am Cherry Alive,' the Little Girl Sang." This is, in a sense, a presentation of Stevens' theme in his partial line "fictive things / Wink as they will" (59), or one might say that the theme of Schwartz's poem is the power of the subjective in the process of making differentiations. Or, it is the freshness of the perception of youth that can, without battle, accept the paradox or the contradiction as the truth of reality. Or, again, it is the ability of the young not only to believe in magic but to exercise it. Finally, it is a singing about the irrepressible confidence of youth, its naïve arrogation to itself of centrality and omniscience.

> "I am red, I am gold, I am green, I am blue,
> I will always be me, I will always be new!" (161)

The next group, "The Kingdom of Poetry," repeats his earlier assertions and advances his thesis only slightly, but it contains two successful poems: "Gold Morning, Sweet Prince" and "Vivaldi." In the former, the substitution of "Gold" for "Good" and "Morning" for "Night," as in the famous phrase from *Hamlet,* is not merely a good example of the punning from which Schwartz was never far, but it also contains the promise of the cycle, which is the promise of rebirth, the seed for which may be found in Schwartz's use and reuse of the word "endless" in his early poetry as well. "Everything is circular," wrote Williams James when he rose from a dream in the small hours of the morning and thought he had the ultimate answer. Schwartz in *his* dream of knowledge returns to the circular, the cycle in which the deeply feared death is always the precursor of birth. In such a belief, it is possible that Schwartz finally gave way to wish and felt the relief and the reward in the acceptance, finally, of a little illusion like a balm. One recalls " ' "Beware of all your desires. You are deceived" ' " (150) from "The Fulfillment" and, from "Gold Morning, Sweet Prince,"

> So there is no choice but the choice of love, unless one
>   chooses
> Never to love, seeking immunity, discovering nothingness.
> (174)

The great wish is faced at last and stated:

> Gold morning, sweet prince, black night has always
>   descended and has always ended. . . . (175)

Schwartz does not hesitate to use phrases from other writers for his own purposes in his line. Sometimes these phrases are punned upon or changed; usually they work, providing an additional richness. In this poem, he borrows from Shakespeare, "*Ripeness is all,*" and this he follows with "*the rest is silence,*" and then adds,

> we are such stuff as love has made us
> And our little life, green, ripe, or rotten, is what it is
> Because of love accepted, rejected, refused and jilted,
>   faded, raided, neglected or betrayed. (174)

Many things are occurring at the same time, in Schwartz the man probably, in Schwartz the poet undoubtedly, and in the symptomatic poetry almost certainly. It is a discourtesy that comment often displaces text. One must carefully select. A matter that must be mentioned, however, is this: on one hand, the poetry seems to be an effort of honesty beyond honesty, and it is immensely successful in communicating the powerful emotion, the insight, and a good part of the experience the poet is attempting to fix for the reader. On the other hand, the mode of the poet, the poetic style, has collapsed, and is becoming, in these later poems, incapable of meeting the demands that are being placed on it. It is, put another way, expanding, becoming gaseous. The minute, the acute, can no longer be expressed with the tool of this style. The building units of the poetry are much greater in size than in the earlier work and cannot be examined with care and with a magnifying glass. One must stand back from the text, if one would see the amorphous outlines of these construction units, very much as one stands back from Allen Ginsberg's poetry, or from the ritual of any aboriginal chant of magic. In this sense, the poems are better read aloud as incantation and exorcism.

There is still another "on the other hand" that must be added—comment on that which seems, from the clues in the poetry, to have been happening to the man and the poet. But first, a quotation from "Vivaldi," an extremely successful poem that purports to be about the music of Vivaldi but that, at the same time, has two other aims: to contain the style that is slipping away like water turning to steam, and to extend and enrich Schwartz's central theme in this section. The poem ends as follows:

> Far from the world of Caesar and Venus, calculation and
>   sensuality, ratiocination and frustration,
> This is the dark city of the hidden innermost wish,
>   The motion beyond emotion,
>   The power beyond and free of power,
>   Beyond beyond within the withness of witness,
> This is the immortality of mortality, this
> Is supreme consciousness,
> The self-forgetting in the self possessed and mastered
>   In the elation of being open to all relation
> No longer watchful, wakeful, guarded, wary, no longer striving
>   and climbing:
> This is the immortality of immortality
>   Deathless and present in the presence of the deathless present.

> This is the grasped reality of reality, moving forward
> Now and forever. (179)

The poem has marginal notes indicating the "time" of each section as if it were a piece of music: "Allegro cantabile," "Scherzo," etc. These directions plus the variation in rhythm occurring in each area as indicated by the directions—not a regular rhythmic change each time but a partial change, an imagined shift—do act as additional elements of formal structure bracing the poem, buttressing the lines.

It is true that this is Eliotic, but it strikes a true note of Schwartz's as well. The similarity to Eliot is really the similarity of most incantatory poetry. Such poetry seeks to move the sensibility up and out of its analytical moorings usually into an undifferentiated ecstasy. The rationale for this effort is that the consciousness dilates, that one gains in awareness as well as in perception. And there is ample reason to suppose that this is the case, so long as widening is not confused with distortion and displacement, both of which can be rewarding but are, nevertheless, of another degree if not nature. This is why there is always the metaphysical import attached to incantatory poetry. They must be hypnotic (as in the dialogue of the theater of the absurd, Ionesco, for example) or they must be exciting (as in a jazz refrain), but neither Eliot nor Schwartz shows such an aim in his verse. Schwartz is, in fact, making a profound effort at seership, and this style has a gyrating rhythm to accommodate the affirmative, mystical, cyclical feeling.

The rise in tone, the elevation, the sense of exultation is, of course, achieved through the rhythm and the repetition. Discounting, just this once, the powerful effect of the connotations as well, one can become shocked at the banality of the naked denotative meanings. The only purpose for such a reduction, since it is hardly the point when considering poetry, is to inquire whether another failure is not in preparation here, one concomitant with the failure in his style. Line by line the above quotation reads something like this: "Far from the world of power and sex where one has to think, where one risks frustration, is one's wishful inner self, which is not subject to external pressures. It is the central life/energy and is not aware of itself. It is happy because it has no ambition, does not need to strive. It is immortal because (probably) we all have it."

What this boils down to is the simple dictum that even when we lose all the rewards, we still have the best thing left—and it can never be taken away from us—our own selves! Now my comment is likely to irritate; on the face of it, it *is* an insulting reduction. Not for a moment can one pretend that this is all there is to the poetry. But it might occasion, at least, a pause to wonder what has happened to the acute conceptual powers exhibited in the early poetry. An answer that occurs is that they are set aside in favor of the titanic emotional struggle that continues. A better answer is given by the totality of the verse, beyond the denotative, and this tells us that the self one is left with is a non-self, that Schwartz in this passage abandons self as it is usually known, and that he now realizes he is only his own experience from moment to moment. But this does not derive from the denotation. It is a triumph of the total poem, set against all the rest of his poetry.

The poet has already spoken of rebirth into love and the love he refers to is selflessness. Here, in the music, the selflessness is incarnate. There is no longer anything so mundane as a love object; both the subject *and* the object disappear. What is left is "The self-forgetting in the self possessed and mastered." Although Schwartz claims, in the lines above, that this is the supreme consciousness, one may be pardoned for substituting understanding for agreement. It is more important to follow this complex, profound, and ingenious exorcism to the very end, keeping in mind the levels involved, realizing that some things that are commented on here occur in the poetry, in the reader, in the author alone. Again one returns to the poet, the poem, the reader, and the world. And one returns, as well, to Schwartz's first story published so many decades before these last poems, the story in which, it was pointed out, three levels of Delmore were occupied with Delmore, his origins, and his future.

By now it should become clear that the poet protests too much, that the word "hope" appears as often as "certainty" and more often than "love." The persuader is trying desperately to persuade himself. The disenchanted is building an enchanted life preserver, literally, and the faster he falls, the more furious the fervor. One can weep at the pathetic—no, tragic—"No longer watchful, wakeful, guarded, wary" not only—and this is the power of the poem—for the poet's special case, but for others and many and everyone. But to understand that, in a sense, this statement from the poem is a lie is more difficult. On the level of his own life (although, at the very same time, this is not a dishonest poem), Schwartz never did forego the watchfulness and wakefulness. The ritual remained a ritual and really did not work, for him at least. The biographical fact is *only* significant here if it helps one to see the nature and the use of such verse, not necessarily its success or failure for the man who wrote it or for the reader. As a matter of fact, one could even say that it was successful for Schwartz, but only because it gave him an upsurge of writing, providing him with a refreshed theme. On this, frankly, his life hung and his sanity. So far as straightforward belief is concerned, however, he was unable to believe, at all, in any way, and not even for a moment.

But he went on weaving the spell. If music can bring this apotheosis of spirit about, then, of course, so can poetry. Perhaps the unkindest comment one could make on the least excellent of these poems, "The Kingdom of Poetry," is that it reads like a spiritual Baedeker. Schwartz is at the middle remove from his material; he is telling about it rather than presenting it. It takes compression rather than an expansion to present it. Some might say, simply, that Schwartz is at base a prose writer who writes here with a strong prose rhythm. Taking into account the early poetry with its highly individual sound and particular Schwartzian rhythm, this estimate seems untenable. "The Kingdom of Poetry" is a paean in which poetry is called "the actuality of possibility" (189) and "the consummation of consciousness in the country of the morning!" (189). Here the language blurs into continuous hyperbole and the effect of repetition is not so much hypnotic as boring. Nevertheless, the desperate exultation prevails.

Schwartz has moved from snow to morning to love to rebirth to selflessness. It is necessary, within the logic of this development, that it be crowned with the sovereignty of poetry, for poetry is "the sunlight of consciousness" (188) and *"The meaning of morning and / The mastery of meaning"* (189). These lines constitute one of the clues that what transpires on paper for the reader cannot be taken as straight confession about what went on in the poet. In this kingdom of poetry, we cannot feel that the abandonment of the old self is accomplished to make way for the new, as the other poems, hostels for the pilgrim on his way up the hill, imply. Into this poem creeps *meaning*—"*The* meaning *of morning / The mastery of* meaning" (emphasis added). This is not "summer knowledge" but meaning in the old sense, meaning that means to the self, the self that holds "mastery" now as before. In the kingdom of poetry one cannot say, "The king is dead, long live the king," because it is the same old king who is ascending the throne. For Schwartz, whatever the degree of salvation vouchsafed him, it came, always, through poetry and with the self, as he said, both "falcon and falconer"; this is still the case. Faced with Schwartz's eloquent claims of mystical experience and seership on the one hand, and this later tribute to poetry on the other, one is hard put not to point out that, most often, true visionaries end in silence. Even the logician Ludwig Wittgenstein closed the *Tractatus* with "Wovon man nicht sprechen kann, darüber muss man schweigen" (189). [What we cannot speak about, we must pass over in silence.]

The rest of the poetry is slippage—reinforcements and admissions. In the lyrical "Hölderlin," Schwartz describes "their voices" as

> Having no more meaning than the fullness of music,
> Chanting from the pure peaks where success,
> Effort and desire are meaningless. . . . (184)

If this is the reinforcing theme, then what is "the mastery of meaning" in "The Kingdom of Poetry?" The admissions follow. Direct statement is used, seeming effort, to make clear some of the psychological bases for the poet's later development. The mask of ecstasy and inducement is wearily dropped and a plaintive public inspection begun.

The fourth section of this part of the book is titled "The Deceptive Present, The Phoenix Year." The poems selected for this section indicate a spiraling downward from the manic to the depressive. This takes the form of a low-key social search of examination that, briefly sustained, then provides a circumstance from which the poet can recoil and toward which he can be defensive. Schwartz has returned to somewhat the same position he held in *Vaudeville for a Princess*. The title of the section is accurate: before the "Phoenix Year" comes the "Deceptive Present." Such a description is a fair preparation for the cynicism—for Schwartz it is worldliness—with which he defends himself in these poems.

"The Foggy, Foggy Blue," which is written to the beat of "The Foggy, Foggy Dew," is a clear expression of this attitude and, interestingly enough, seems to appeal to most young people. The first stanza follows:

> When I was a young man, I loved to write poems
>> And I called a spade a spade
> And the only only thing that made me sing
>> Was to lift the masks at the masquerade.
> I took them off my own face,
>> I took them off the others too
> And the only only wrong in all my song
>> Was the view that I knew what was true. (206)

Truthfully, his second stanza admits that he is older and tireder and "the tasks with the masks are quite trying." He reviews his past when he "tried to be less starry-eyed" but only became confused, "Forgetting what was false and what was true" (206). In the final stanza he reveals that he is now beyond the true and the false. He has abandoned his search for the truth, the drive to pare away the false or the superfluous. He is giving in to the situation in which "most falsehoods are true." He has lost the need to judge, to be "naïve and stern." He is giving up the battle in favor of the noncritical affirmation.

> Let live and believe, I say,
> The only only thing is to believe in everything. . . . (206)

And why?

> Because it has occurred to me
> That the masks are more true than the faces. . . . (206)

This can be taken as an insight into the image projections by which people present themselves and receive others. It is reminiscent of Eliot's "To prepare a face to meet the faces that you meet" (4). It implies that we live in a world of fictions delivered to us by symbols and that the uncovering is merely the exchanging of one mask for another. The young people see in it a cynical expression of disappointment. But in the spiral of Schwartz's progression, it can, on the surface, be taken to show that he is moving on to a point where he will be willing to drop his defensiveness, to give up the masking and the unmasking, to go on, albeit wearily, to a new and saving level of acceptance. But the tone belies this and the last line, "It's more fun and safer that way!" implies, in that it is a motion from seriousness to fun, that once again the poet recognizes the correct (healthful?) formula, but cannot really give in to it any more than he can treat himself with lightness and gayety. "I Did Not Know the Spoils of Joy" in the same section has the same tone of forced gayety; it even ends, "How I am glad that I exist!" (209), yet it carries the same message.

The poem "The Deceptive Present, The Phoenix Year" adds another association to the word "deceptive." The present is deceptive because it gives the impression, for the moment, of existing forever.

> All winter, the trees had been
> Silent soldiers, a vigil of woods. . . . (212)

The winter had seemed forever: "Barbed wire sharp against the ice-white sky" (212). The poet asks, then, who could have believed in the spring that the spring will come when all is "Wet, white, ice, wooden, dulled and dead, brittle or frozen" (212)? This is the nature of the deceptive present. Yet there is hope because "The reality of spring and of birth" (212) is certain to return. And this is the meaning of "The Phoenix Year." The passing moment seems eternal and possesses in itself only stasis, but the year, the cycle, as in other mystical writing, noticeably Eliot's, promises renewal. Again, symbolically, the winter with its soldiers and barbed wire refers to Schwartz's defensive, isolated past in which the ego shored itself up and was consumed to protect itself, loveless, and worse, unloving. But the phoenix year, the cycle, brings a discarding of the defenses and an opening up to the "green warm opulence of summer" (212) and the inexhaustible vitality and immortality of the earth—a new humility for the poet if it were really accepted, but one supposes it is merely assumed.

In "The Conclusion" he offers this explanation:

> The furs which love in all its warmth discloses
> Become the fires of pride and are betrayed
> By those *whom love has terrified and pride has made afraid.*
> (201; italics added)

In the poem "All of the Fruits Had Fallen," the name of which implies that summer is over and with it "summer knowledge," Schwartz reviews his situation:

> I wished for the innocence
> Of my stars and my stones and my trees
> All the brutality and inner sense
> A dog and a bird possess . . .
>
> . . . .
> —Until, in the dim window glass,
> The fog or cloud of my face
> Showed me my fear at last! (205)

The last section of the book, "The Phoenix Choir," is short and appears on the whole, needlessly separated from the prior section. It contains several poems from previous volumes, one from *Genesis*, which is here called "Lincoln," and the well-known "Starlight Like Intuition Pierced the Twelve,"

first published in book form in *Vaudeville for a Princess*. There are three
more or less prose poems of biblical derivation: "Abraham," "Sarah," and
"Jacob." These mark no definitive points of development but are fond com-
pilations and restatements of attitudes and insights presented in previous
work and commented upon in this study. In three poems, he reworks his
doubts and asserts his hope in the cyclical nature of things: "Once and for
All" confesses that his original loyalty to Apollo and subsequent default
into the ranks of Dionysus (an admission again of guilt) was an error in the
sense that no such dichotomy exists and that he has moved on to a position
discovering "the opulence hidden in the dark depths and glittering heights
of reality" (222). "The River Was the Emblem of All Beauty: All" revivi-
fies the conventional symbol of cycle as background to the poet's pitiful
performance in public:

> Could they have seen how my faces were
> Bonfires of worship and vigil, blazes of adoration and hope
> —Surely they would have laughed again, renewed their
> scorn. . . .   (228–29)

His defensiveness, his paranoia, nags him. But finally, stone-cold and
sober, in one of his last poems of the book, "The Fear and the Dread of the
Mind of Others," he writes:

> Knowing their certainty that I was only
> A monument, a monster who had fallen in love
> With himself alone, how could I have
> Told them what was in me, within my heart trembling and
> passionate . . . ?
> . . . .
> Do you hear? do you see? Do you understand me now,
> and how
> The words for what is my heart do not exist? (227–28)

Works Cited

Bacon, Delia. *The Philosophy of The Plays of Shakspere Unfolded.* Preface Nathaniel Hawthorne. Boston: Ticknor and Fields, 1857.

Eliot, T. S. *Collected Poems, 1909–1962.* New York: Harcourt, Brace & World, Inc., 1963.

Gide, André. *Lafcadio's Adventures.* New York: Vintage Books, 1953.

Giraudoux, Jean. *Tiger at the Gates: A Play in Two Acts.* Trans. Christopher Fry. New York: Samuel French, 1955.

Hardy, Thomas. "The Oxen." *The Pocket Book of Modern Verse.* Ed. Oscar Williams. New York: Washington Square Press, 1966.

Ralli, Augustus. *A History of Shakespearian Criticism.* Vol. II. Oxford: Oxford University Press, 1932.

Robinson, Edwin Arlington. "From *Tristram.*" *Twentieth Century American Writing.* Ed. William T. Stafford. New York: Odyssey Press, 1965.

Schwartz, Delmore. *Genesis.* New York: New Directions, 1943.

———. *In Dreams Begin Responsibilities.* Norfolk, Conn.: New Directions, 1938.

———. "Paris and Helen." *New Directions in Prose and Poetry.* 6. Ed. James Laughlin. Norfolk, Conn.: New Directions, 1941. 194–219.

———. *Shenandoah.* Norfolk, Conn.: New Directions, 1941.

———. *Summer Knowledge: New and Selected Poems, 1938–1958.* Garden City, N.Y.: Doubleday & Co., 1959.

———. *Vaudeville for a Princess and Other Poems.* New York: New Directions, 1950.

Stevens, Wallace. *The Collected Poems of Wallace Stevens.* New York: Alfred A. Knopf, 1954.

———. *Letters of Wallace Stevens.* Sel. and Ed. Holly Stevens. New York: Alfred A. Knopf, 1966.

Tate, Allen. "Sonnets at Christmas." *A Pocket Book of Modern Verse.* Ed. Oscar Williams. New York: Washington Square Press, 1958.

Wittgenstein, Ludwig. *Tractatus Logico-Philosophicus.* London: Routledge & K. Paul, 1960.

Yeats, William Butler. "Crazy Jane Talks with the Bishop." *The Collected Poems of W. B. Yeats.* New York: Macmillan, 1956.

About the Author

Robert H. Deutsch
1915–1983
Poet, Scholar, Professor

Robert Deutsch was a man of letters. He founded the Wallace Stevens Society and was editor-in-chief of *The Wallace Stevens Journal* from 1977 until his death in December 1983. He was a conflicted man, who wrote "adulthood is the resolution of opposites." He was profound, funny, elegant, and coarse, and he lived his contradictions bravely. He loved all his wives, in his way, and despite themselves, they all loved him. He delighted in stirring things up and he snubbed death. He chose the singers for his funeral and left a refrigerator full of cakes for his friends to eat as they remembered him—cakes ordered in the middle of the night on one of his last days on earth, cakes from the company Harry and David, because that is what his sons were named. Then he left his favorite humidor to two rival professors.